# Indian Games and Dances with Native Songs

# Indian Games and Dances with Native Songs

ARRANGED FROM AMERICAN INDIAN
CEREMONIALS AND SPORTS

BY

## ALICE C. FLETCHER

*Introduction by Helen Myers*

University of Nebraska Press
Lincoln and London

Introduction copyright 1994 by the University of Nebraska Press
Manufactured in the United States of America

The paper in this book meets the minimum requirements of American National Standard for Information Sciences—Permanence of Paper for Printed Library Materials, ANSI z39.48-1984

First Bison Book printing: 1994
most recent printing indicated by the last digit below:
10   9   8   7   6   5   4   3   2   1

Library of Congress Cataloging-in-Publication Data
Fletcher, Alice C. (Alice Cunningham), 1838–1923.
Indian games and dances with native songs: arranged from American Indian ceremonials and sports / by Alice C. Fletcher: introduction by Helen Myers.
p.   cm.
Originally published: Boston: C.C. Birchard, 1915. With new introd.
"Bison book."
Includes bibliographical references.
ISBN 0-8032-6886-6 (pbk.)
1. Indians of North America—Games.   2. Indians of North America—Music.   3. Indian dance—North America.   I. Title.
E98.G2F6   1994
394'.3'09701—dc20
94-31508
CIP

Reprinted from the original edition published in 1915 by C. C. Birchard & Company, Boston.

DEDICATED TO

THE YOUTH OF AMERICA

# INTRODUCTION

by Helen Myers

aided by Elsie Myers-Stainton

"Fourfold deep lie my roots with the land;
Clad in green, bearing fruit. Lo! here I stand
Pluck and eat, life for life, behold, I give!
Shout with joy, dance and sing with all that live."
                                        Ritual Song

In the early years of the twentieth century, long before the
plight of American Indians in the United States had become a
national concern, a friend of those Indian tribes called them
what they now request as their true designation. That honored
name is Native American; that friend was Alice Cunningham
Fletcher (1838–1923).

Alice Fletcher has earned for herself a special place among
American anthropologists. She was one of the first to pay attention to Native American music, and most important she listened with a sympathetic ear to the sounds she heard. Born in
1838, at the age of forty-three she was so inspired by a self-im-
posed goal that she determined to visit the very Sioux Indians
who five years before had defeated George Custer at the Little
Big Horn. Eventually, for a time, she made her home with
them.

## Indian Games and Dances

Her rapport with the Indians who received her as a guest and cared for her when she was ill led her naturally to call them what they are—natives of America. Her insights into their culture, her understanding of their traditions, and perception of their feelings are now as pertinent as ever. Her dedication of *Indian Games and Dances with Native Songs,* her last book, originally published in 1915, still stands: "Dedicated to the Youth of America." She hoped that all Americans would listen to the Native American songs and come to understand the people who sang those songs and cherish them. Knowledge of the dances and games too, she writes, might help people to "recognize, enjoy and share in the spirit of the olden life upon this continent" (p. xxii). Her purpose in writing this book, she says, was "to find some way by which I could help to make available to others the voice I had heard, and thereby restore to our hills and valleys their lost human element" (pp. xxi–xxii).

Her acknowledgment to the musical director of the Morris High School of New York City "for assistance in the preparation of this book" (p. xxii) shows the direction of her efforts.

Here Alice Fletcher has provided "adaptations" (p. 1) of Indian ceremonies and sports so that others, particularly the young, might participate and perhaps share the feelings that Native Americans have for their land and all nature, and which are expressed and acted out in these songs and dances. In this way a better understanding of the native American "consciousness of oneness with nature" (p. 3) might be realized: "I had learned to hear the echoes of a time when every living thing upon this land and even the varied overshadowing skies had its voice, a voice that was attentively heard and devoutly heeded by the ancient people of America" (p. xxi).

The games, dances, and songs that Fletcher selected to include in this volume span the country: the dances and songs come from the Omaha, Osage, and Pawnee tribes; those titled "Calling the Flowers," from the Indians of the North Pacific Coast; "Appeal for a Clear Sky," from the tribes of the Mississippi Valley. The "Omaha Festival of Joy" includes dances and songs from a region north of the present city of Omaha, Nebraska.

The games that Fletcher chose, which include songs, "appear to be the direct and natural outgrowth of aboriginal institutions in America" (p. 63), she says, quoting Dr. Stewart Culin (Bureau of American Ethnology, Vol. 24, p. 32), an authority on Indian games. "There is no evidence," Culin says, "that these games were imported into America at any time either before or after the conquest." And "traces of the articles used for them have been found in the oldest remains on this continent" (p. 63).

Fletcher assembled games from tribes of the northeastern states, the Atlantic coast, the Great Lakes, the southern states, the North Pacific coast, and California; Pueblo Indians and Plains Indians; and specifically the Cherokee, Omaha, Nez Percé (Idaho), Otoe, Ponca, Pawnee, Chippewa (Minnesota), and Marecopa (Arizona).

Games of chance and guessing came chiefly under the headings of athletic sports. Guessing games or games of choice, in the games-of-chance group, are usually accompanied by singing. Games of chance that depend upon the random fall of something like dice are generally played in silence.

Twenty song notations are provided to go with dances, eight songs to go with games, and two for name songs. All the songs are notated on a conventional Western treble stave, with the key and time signatures, and bar lines indicated. A single line of melody is given and no suggestion of harmonization. So Fletcher in her last book did not use the harmonic method devised by her early collaborator, John Comfort Fillmore (1843–98), a teacher at the Milwaukee School of Music who had studied at Oberlin and in Leipzig, Germany. In her first major publication *A Study of Omaha Indian Music* (1893; reprint, Lincoln: University of Nebraska Press, 1994), Fletcher devotes considerable space to Fillmore's ninety-two arrangements of Indian melodies as well as his nineteen-page essay, "A Report on the Structural Peculiarities of the Music." In a number of Fletcher's early works Fillmore illustrated his now discredited theory of "latent harmony," a notion whereby there was a common harmonic basis for all music. Indian melodies implied harmonies that could be supplied by musically trained Westerners. Many of Fletcher's early transcriptions thus appear in four-part harmony, arranged by Fillmore and scored by him for the piano. In her later writings, including the present work, Fletcher abandoned this idea, together with its evolutionistic implications (Indian music as a simple precursor to a more sophisticated Western system of harmony).

In two of the game songs in the present volume, places for drumbeats are marked. In one name song, places for handclaps are indicated, and the text instructs: "All present should then join in singing the following song, clapping their hands as beats to the music" (p. 133–34):

> ". . . . Singing we go, way ha way ho!
> Dancing also, way ha way ho!
> No one more merry than we, way ha way ho!"

The book also includes four diagrams to illustrate the games.

In a third part entitled "Indian Names," Fletcher deals with the ceremonies for bestowing names—a child's name given when inducted into the tribe (at three or four years of age) or the new name a man may receive after demonstrating special "ability or strength of character" (p. 126). A ritual is enacted for each newborn infant, revealing how a child, a person, is regarded as part of all nature. The child, the "new life" (p. 123), is presented to the cosmos, and "all the powers of the heaven and of the earth were invoked to render aid" (p. 121).

"Ho! Ye Sun, Moon, Stars . . . Ho! Ye Winds, Clouds, Rain, Mist. . . . Ho! Ye Hills, Valleys, Rivers, Lakes, Trees, Grasses. . . . Ho! Ye Birds. . . . Ho! Ye Animals. . . . I bid you hear me! Into your midst has come a new life. . . . Consent ye, consent ye all, I implore! Make its path smooth" (pp. 120–21). The priest summoned intones the five stanzas, with each refrain, at the door of the tent where the child is.

Fletcher rounds out her presentation with lists of Indian names for boys and for girls and for camps, as rendered by the Omaha, Ponca, Osage, and Dakota tribes, all of them share a language group.

Fletcher's detailed description of the "Festival of Joy" is a treasure: "For centuries the home of the Omaha tribe has been in the region now known as the State of Nebraska, north of the city which bears their name. There they dwelt in permanent villages, surrounded by their garden plots of corn, beans, squashes, etc. From these villages every year in June all the tribe except the sick and infirm went forth to follow the buffalo herds in order to obtain their supply of meat pelts. . . . It was at the close of this great tribal hunt, when food and clothing had been secured, while Summer lingered and the leaves had not yet begun to fall, so that brightness was still over the land, that this Festival of Joy took place" (p. 54).

Influence on American Composers

Fletcher was proud to say that some of her Indian transcriptions, published before the turn of the century, "have been used by different composers and the musical message sent far and wide" (p. 4). La Flesche also, in summing up her accomplishments, mentioned her influence upon composers of the day.

The first was Edward MacDowell (1860–1908) with his "Indian Suite for Orchestra" (Op. 48, 1890).

Arthur Farwell (1872–1952), encouraged by MacDowell, first worked with Indian music between 1900 and 1904. Although a prolific composer with many interests, he became known as a collector and arranger of American Indian music. A set of piano pieces, *Impressions of the Wa-Wan Ceremony* of the Omahas appeared in 1905. His string quartet, "The Hako" (1922), was based on Indian ritual songs. In these and other works derived from Indian music, Farwell was able to preserve an essential simplicity. In 1901 he founded the Wa-Wan Press after failing to find a publisher for his *American Indian Melodies*. The press published works of contemporary American composers as well as the *Wa-Wan Press Monthly*, often with introductions to the musicians as well as articles on music by Farwell, until 1912. In his writings he spoke up for the musical expression of American diversity. In the first American sound-and-light show (in Central Park, New York City, 1916), as producer, he introduced extended vocal technique as used by American Indians.

Around 1908, Charles Wakefield Cadman (1881–1946) read the Fletcher and La Flesche articles about the Omahas, and in 1909 he spent the summer with La Flesche on the Omaha reservation and the Winnebago. He recorded tribal songs there and later in the year arranged and published *Four American Indian Songs*, with words by Nellie Richmond Eberhart. Of these, two were sung widely; "At Dawning" and "From the Land of the Sky-Blue Water" could be heard, accompanied by piano, in many homes for decades. In 1910 an Omaha Indian, Princess Tsianina Redfeather, cooperated with Cadman in a series of lecture-performances, "American Indian Music Talk," which toured in Europe as well as the United States. His opera, *Shanewis*, based on the life of the Princess, was a great success at the Metropolitan Opera in 1918 and again in 1919. Other of his compositions include the unperformed opera *The Land of the Misty Water* (1909), for which acknowledgment was given to La Flesche; instrumental pieces entitled *Idealized Indian Themes* (performed 1912) and *To a Vanishing Race* (1925); and the vocal pieces *From Wigwam and Teepee,* a song cycle on Indian themes (1914).

Charles T. Griffes (1884–1920), a prolific composer who experimented widely, also turned to Indian music in *Two Sketches Based on Indian Themes* (premier, 1920).

## The Fletcher–La Flesche Collection

Early on, Fletcher listened and notated her Indian songs out on Indian lands, chiefly Nebraska and Idaho. Later she notated songs of visiting Indians at her home in Washington D.C. Eventually she and La Flesche used the wax cylinder of the Edison phonograph for recording, and later transcribing, the words and tunes.

By the fall of 1888 she and La Flesche had collected more than a hundred songs. By the early 1900s they had amassed more than five hundred cylinders. Scholars consider that the Fletcher and La Flesche recordings are of exceptional quality. Transferred in 1948 from the National Archives, the Library of Congress has 237 cylinders of Native American music credited to Fletcher and 254 to La Flesche. All have been transferred to and preserved on magnetic tape.

Selected historical recordings from the Fletcher/La Flesche Collection were issued in 1985 by the Library of Congress on 33 1/3 LP record with accompanying booklet, "Omaha Indian Music," edited by Dorothy Sara Lee and Maria La Vigna and produced by the American Folklife Center in cooperation with the Omaha Tribal Council (AFC L71).

Fletcher hoped for continued interest in Indian traditions. There is no lessening of that interest. "The current renaissance of interest in the American Indian is in large measure related to our critical concern. In our search for ourselves we are beginning to look to the American Indian in a manner never attempted before. We wish to know who the Indian was and is, by what values he lived, and the nature of his special relationship with his natural environment. . . . If the search is sincere, it is possible that men may learn from the Indian's legacy and example" (Joseph Epes Brown, *The North American Indians*).

An obituary for Alice Fletcher noted that she "made unusually important contributions to our knowledge of the inner spirit and beauty of the Indian's concepts. . . . Her collection of data was expedited by the simplicity of her dealings with the Indians and her entire sympathy with them. She was a friend among friends, and all her inquiries were answered freely and with confidence as one of the family. Such conditions are not often granted to anthropological investigators and for this reason much information on various lines of Indian life are irreparably lost. . . . As an interpreter of the Indian Miss Fletcher ranks among the highest. Mildly, peaceably, yet with great fortitude, she did what she could to advance the cause of science and science is her debtor" (Walter Hough, *American Anthropologist,* vol. 25, p. 24).

## The Life of Alice Fletcher

Alice Cunningham Fletcher was born in 1838 in Cuba, where her parents had gone hoping to benefit her father's health, but he died the next year of tuberculosis. The young Miss Fletcher attended exclusive schools, traveled in Europe, and taught at several private schools. With a pleasing voice and attractive manner, she became successful on the lecture circuits, and thereby supported herself. While preparing lectures on ancient Americans, she met Frederick W. Putnam, director of the Peabody Museum at Harvard, who encouraged her to continue anthropological study and stressed a scientific approach to her work. For a time she was an assistant at the Museum.

Fletcher met Francis La Flesche (1857–1932) at a Boston fund-raising event in 1879. He was a son of Omaha Chief Joseph La Flesche. Susette, Francis's sister, was interpreter for Standing Bear, the Ponca chief. Along with Thomas Henry Tibbles, a Nebraska journalist who later married Susette, they were touring the East to protest removal of the Poncas from the Dakota Territory. Having lectured chiefly on material gathered in libraries, Fletcher now wished for first-hand information. She contacted Susette and Tibbles early in 1881, and during the summer, they arranged for her to return with them that fall, in a wooden wagon, to the Omaha reservation in Nebraska and then on into Sioux territory. This was the beginning. The result is described by her mentor, Frederick Putnam, in his "Editorial Note" to *A Study of Omaha Indian Music:* "Her long residence among the Indians and her success in winning their love and perfect confidence have enabled her to penetrate the meaning of many things which to an ordinary observer of Indian life are incomprehensible" (p. xxi).

Again early in 1882, while working for the Omahas in Washington, she frequently sought Francis La Flesche's help. They helped each other thereafter for more than forty years. While he was engaged in research for the Bureau of American Ethnology, Fletcher was herself involved in many important projects. She continued to write. She became an intermediary between government agencies and Indian tribes. She was asked to administer settlements of controversial land allotments. She sponsored educational projects for Indians. She was a vice president of the American Association for the Advancement of Science (1896), a founding member of the American Anthropological Association (1902), president of the American Folklore Society (1905), and was on the editorial board of the *American Anthropologist* (1899–1916).

In 1892 she moved into a house that had been bought for her on 214 First Street SE in Washington D.C. This home became a gathering place for intellectuals, among them Ainsworth Spofford, once President Lincoln's secretary and later Librarian of Congress. Fletcher lived there, with La Flesche, until her death in 1923.

At her death, aged eighty-five, Alice Fletcher had been in the public eye for more than forty years—as lecturer, author, government official, anthropologist, and musicologist. She worked hard and welcomed the rewards, chiefly recognition of her accomplishments, which at other times she felt was denied her. She was brave, determined, resourceful, and most important of all, she left a legacy of some forty-six writings on aspects of Indian life and music.

\* \* \*

From "Alice C. Fletcher," *Science*, vol. 58, no. 1494 (17 August 1923), p. 115.

"In the year 1881 there appeared on the Omaha reservation, in Nebraska, a white woman. She visited the Indians in their homes and began to make friends with them. At first they were not disposed to talk, but after a time it occurred to one to ask: "Why are you here?' She replied: 'I came to learn, if you will let me, something about your tribal organization, social customs, tribal rites, traditions and songs. Also to see if I can help you in any way.'

"At the suggestion of help the faces of the Indians brightened with hope. The Indian continued: 'You have come at a time when we are in distress. We have learned that the "land paper" given us by the Great Father does not make us secure in our homes; that we could be ousted and driven to the Indian Territory as the Poncas were. We want a "strong paper." We are told that we can get one through an act of Congress. Can you help us?

"The little woman replied: 'Bring me your "land paper" and come prepared to tell me about your home and the size of the land you have in cultivation. Come soon.' The news spread and the Indians came. . . .

" . . . This brave, unselfish woman was Alice C. Fletcher, whom the Omahas learned to love.

" . . . Miss Fletcher came to Washington to help push the bill through [to secure land titles for the Omahas]. It passed both houses, was approved August 7, 1882, and became law.

"In April, 1883, Miss Fletcher was appointed special agent to carry out the provisions of the law. When she was about to begin her work the older members of the tribe came together for consultation as to how they could best express their gratitude for what she had done for the tribe. They decided to perform for her the ancient calumet ceremony, although it was not customary to give it informally. A notice was given to the people to come, and on the day appointed many came and assembled in an earth lodge. The calumets were set up in their sacred place, and when Miss Fletcher entered as the honored guest the house became silent. Three men arose and took up the symbolic pipes (the calumets) and the lynx skin on which they rested; then standing side by side, they sang softly the opening song. At the close the three men turned, and facing the people, who sat in a wide circle, sang a joyful song as they moved around the circle, waving the sacred pipes over their heads. Song after song they sang for their friend, of the joy and happiness that would follow when men learned to live together in peace. When the evening was over they told Miss Fletcher that she was free to study this or any other of their tribal rites.

"Miss Fletcher carried on her ethnological researches among the Omaha, Pawnee, Winnebago, Sioux, Nez Pierce and other tribes she studied. . . . Many of the ceremonial songs collected by Miss Fletcher have been used as themes by American composers, notably Cadman, Farwell and others. . . .

"This great friend of the Indians was born in Cuba on the 15th day of March, 1838; on the evening of April 6, 1923, she passed away in her home, in Washington, D.C."

Francis La Flesche

## Bibliography

Brady, Erika, Maria La Vigna, Dorothy Sara Lee, and Thomas Vennum Jr., *The Federal Cylinder Project: A Guide to Field Cylinder Collections in Federal Agencies*. vol. 1: *Introduction and Inventory. Studies in American Folklife*, no. 3, vol. 1. Washington DC: Library of Congress, 1984.

Densmore, Frances. "The Study of Indian Music in the Nineteenth Century." *American Anthropologist* 29 (1927), 77–86.

Fletcher, Alice, "Historical Sketch of the Omaha Tribe of Indians in Nebraska." Washington DC: Bureau of Indian Affairs, 1885.

———. "Leaves from My Omaha Note-book." *Journal of American Folk-Lore* 2 (1889), 219–26.

———. "Indian Songs: Personal Studies of Indian Life." *The Century Magazine* 47 (January 1894), 421–31.

———. *Indian Story and Song from North America*. Boston: Small, Maynard, 1900; reprinted with Introduction by Helen Myers, Lincoln: University of Nebraska Press, 1994.

———. *The Hako: A Pawnee Ceremony*. With James R. Murie. Smithsonian Institution, Bureau of American Ethnology, 22nd Annual Report. Washington DC, 1904. 372 pp.

———. *The Omaha Tribe*. With Francis La Flesche. Smithsonian Institution, Bureau of American Ethnology, 27th Annual Report, 1905–1906. Washington DC, 1911. 672 pp.

———. *A Study of Omaha Indian Music*. Aided by Francis La Flesche and John C. Fillmore. *Archaeological and Ethnological Papers*, Peabody Museum of Archaeology and Ethnology, 1 (1893), 237–87;

reprinted with Introduction by Helen Myers, Lincoln: University of Nebraska Press, 1994.

Hough, Walter. "Alice Cunningham Fletcher." *American Anthropologist* 25 (1923), 254–58.

La Flesche, Francis. "Alice C. Fletcher." *Science* 58, no. 1494 (17 August 1923), 115.

Lee, Dorothy Sara. "North America 1. Native American." In *Ethnomusicology: Historical and Regional Studies,* ed. Helen Myers. London: Macmillan Press, 1993, 19–36.

Lee, Dorothy Sara, and Maria La Vigna, eds. *Omaha Indian Music: Historical Recordings from the Fletcher/La Flesche Collection.* (Booklet accompanying LP disk AFC L71). Washington DC: Library of Congress, 1985.

Lummis, Charles F. "In Memoriam: Alice C. Fletcher." *Art and Archaeology* 16 (1923), 75–76.

Mark, Joan. *Four Anthropologists.* New York: Science History Publications, 1981.

———. *A Stranger in Her Native Land: Alice Fletcher and the American Indians.* Lincoln: University of Nebraska Press, 1988.

Merriam, Alan. *The Anthropology of Music.* Evanston: Northwestern University Press, 1964.

Myers, Helen, ed. *Ethnomusicology: An Introduction.* London: Macmillan Press, 1992.

———. *Ethnomusicology: Historical and Regional Studies.* London: Macmillan, 1993.

Nettl, Bruno. *North American Indian Musical Styles.* Philadelphia: American Folklore Society, 1954.

Welch, Rebecca Hancock. "Alice Cunningham Fletcher, Anthropologist and Indian Rights Reformer." Ph.D. diss., George Washington University, 1980.

Wilkins, Thurman. "Alice Cunningham Fletcher." In *Notable American Women,* ed. Edward T. James, Janet Wilson James, and Paul Boyer. Cambridge: Harvard University Press, 1971.

# PREFACE

THIS little book took its rise in the following experience that came to me many years ago when living with the Indians in their homes and pursuing my ethnological studies:

One day I suddenly realized with a rude shock that, unlike my Indian friends, I was an alien, a stranger in my native land; its fauna and flora had no fond, familiar place amid my mental imagery, nor did any thoughts of human aspiration or love give to its hills and valleys the charm of personal companionship. I was alone, even in my loneliness.

Time went on. The outward aspect of nature remained the same, but imperceptibly a change had been wrought in me until I no longer felt alone in a strange, silent country. I had learned to hear the echoes of a time when every living thing upon this land and even the varied overshadowing skies had its voice, a voice that was attentively heard and devoutly heeded by the ancient people of America. Henceforth, to me the plants, the trees, the clouds and all things had become vocal with human hopes, fears and supplications.

When I realized how much closer because of this change I had been drawn to our land, how much greater had become my enjoyment of nature, the desire arose to find some way by which I could help to make audible to others the voice I had heard, and thereby restore to our hills and valleys their lost human element.  Impelled by this purpose I have arranged these dances and games with native songs in order that our young people may recognize, enjoy and share in the spirit of the olden life upon this continent.

My obligations are due to Mr. Francis La Flesche of the U. S. Bureau of American Ethnology and to Mr. Edwin S. Tracy, Musical Director of the Morris High School of New York City, for assistance in the preparation of this book.

ALICE  C.  FLETCHER

# CONTENTS

PAGE

PREFACE . . . . . . . . . . . . . . . . . .   V

INTRODUCTION . . . . . . . . . . . . . . .   I

SONG AND DANCE AMONG THE INDIANS . . . . . . . .   4

## PART I
### DANCES AND SONGS

THE LIFE OF THE CORN (a Drama in Five Dances) . . . .   9
    Introduction . . . . . . . . . . . . .   9
    Dance I.  The Corn Speaks . . . . . . . . .   11
    Dance II.  Planting the Corn . . . . . . . .   15
    Dance III.  The Corn Springs Up . . . . . . .   23
    Dance IV.  The Fields are Ready . . . . . . .   30
    Dance V.  Honor to Mother Corn . . . . . . .   35
CALLING THE FLOWERS . . . . . . . . . . . .   40
APPEAL FOR CLEAR SKY . . . . . . . . . . . .   48
THE HÉ-DE WA-CHI (An Omaha Festival of Joy) . . . .   54

## PART II
### GAMES

INTRODUCTION . . . . . . . . . . . . . . .   63

#### HAZARD GAMES

INTRODUCTORY NOTE . . . . . . . . . . . . .   67
PA-TOL STICK . . . . . . . . . . . . . . .   68
PLUM STONE . . . . . . . . . . . . . . . .   71

GUESSING GAMES

PAGE

INTRODUCTORY NOTE . . . . . . . . . . . . . . . 73

PU-IN . . . . . . . . . . . . . . . . . . . . . 74

ATÁ-A-KUT . . . . . . . . . . . . . . . . . . 76

HAND GAME . . . . . . . . . . . . . . . . . . . 80

HIDING THE DISKS . . . . . . . . . . . . . . . . 84

I-OU'-TIN . . . . . . . . . . . . . . . . . . . 88

BALL GAMES

INTRODUCTION . . . . . . . . . . . . . . . . . 98

BALL AND RACKET . . . . . . . . . . . . . . . . 98

TA-BÉ . . . . . . . . . . . . . . . . . . . . 102

DOUBLE-BALL . . . . . . . . . . . . . . . . . 105

HOOP AND JAVELIN . . . . . . . . . . . . . . . 108

FOLLOW MY LEADER . . . . . . . . . . . . . . . 114

# PART III
## INDIAN NAMES

INTRODUCTION . . . . . . . . . . . . . . . . . 117

PRESENTING THE CHILD TO THE COSMOS . . . . . . . 120

GIVING THE CHILD A NAME . . . . . . . . . . . . 123

BESTOWING A NEW NAME . . . . . . . . . . . . . 126

TAKING AN INDIAN NAME IN CAMP . . . . . . . . . 132

INDIAN NAMES FOR BOYS . . . . . . . . . . . . . 135

INDIAN NAMES FOR GIRLS . . . . . . . . . . . . 137

INDIAN NAMES FOR CAMPS . . . . . . . . . . . . 139

# PART I

## DANCES

# INDIAN GAMES AND DANCES WITH NATIVE SONGS

## INTRODUCTION

THE adaptations from Indian ceremonies and sports here offered will enable those who take part in them to follow in happy mood some of the paths of expression that were opened long ago by thoughtful men and women as they lived, worked and played on this land in undisturbed intimacy with nature. Some of the thoughts bred of this intimacy find their expression in these dances and games, and it may help toward a better understanding of them and their spirit to tell briefly how the Indian looked upon and regarded his relation to nature.

The natives of America thought of the cosmos as a unit that was throbbing with the same life-force of which they were conscious within themselves; a force that gave to the rocks and hills their stable, unchanging character; to every living thing on land or water the power of growth and of movement; to man the ability to think, to will and to bring to pass. This universal and permeating life-force was always thought of as sacred, powerful, like a god. To it a name was given that varied in the different languages; in the Omaha tongue it was called Wakon'da. Through Wakon'da all things in nature were related and more or less interdependent, the sky, the earth, the animals and men.

Nature was, in a sense, the manifestation of Wakon'da, consequently it was regarded as something more than the means by which physical life was sustained and became the religious and ethical instructor of man.

All food came from the earth; the wild fruits, the roots, the cultivated maize, these and the animals all derived their living power from Wakon'da and yielded their life to man that he might live and be strong. Therefore, the hunt was conducted with ceremonies in which the bounty of Wakon'da was formally recognized, and when food was eaten thanks were offered to this unseen power. The Indian lived in the open and watched with reverent attention the changing aspects of his environment. To him nothing was without significance, for all things were imbued with powers from Wakon'da and could convey lessons or admonitions to be heeded by the individual and by the people in their social life.

For example: the Indian noted the unfailing recurrence of day and night and that upon the regularity with which one followed the other all creatures relied, while man depended upon this constancy to carry out any given purpose. From thoughts upon this natural phenomenon and its effects on the actions of men, ideas arose that led the Indian to the conception of truth, that something, as between man and man, that can be depended on both in word and in deed. "Thus," the old men said, "Wakon'da taught us the necessity of truthfulness, if we would live peacefully together." Other natural aspects, as the storm, with its terrifying thunder and destructive lightning, and the passing of the clouds revealing the blue sky, when the birds renewed their song, seemed to picture to the Indian the devastation of war and the happiness of peace. Again, the tree, compacted of many parts, suggested how the tribe could be made to stand and become strong.

So it came to pass that as the ancient people looked about and thought on what they saw, they gradually formulated ceremonies and adopted symbols in order to express what they came to believe. All their rites, their vocations, their pleasures were born, practiced and enjoyed under the arching skies, and were permeated, as by a vital spirit, with an unquestioning consciousness of oneness with nature.

We shall not be false to any great truths that have been revealed to us concerning the world in which we live, if we listen to the olden voice, an unseen heritage of our bounteous land, as it sings of man's unity with nature. May they who join in these dances and games catch their vital spirit and learn to feel at home with the winds, the clouds, the fields and the woods.

# SONG AND DANCE AMONG THE INDIANS

## The Song

WHILE studying Indian life and thought through the sharing, as far as possible, of native conditions, I discovered Indian music. In the loneliness that naturally belonged to my circumstances this discovery was like finding a flower hidden in a tangle hard to penetrate. I had heard Indians "singing," but the noise of the drum, the singers' stress of voice, so overlaid the little song that its very existence was not even suspected. Circumstances at length arose, incident to my convalescence after a long illness, when, to give me pleasure, my Indian friends came and sang softly to me, without the drum. Great was my surprise to hear music; to be told that I was listening to the same songs that the earnest men and women had previously sung but which for me had been buried under a tumultuous din. Thenceforth my ears were opened and never again, no matter how confusing the conditions, did I fail to catch the hidden melody. As my appreciation of the value of Indian music grew, I determined to gather and to preserve these wild flowers of song. I wanted them not merely as a contribution to the study of music but that they might help to vibrate the chords that belong to a common humanity.

Of the songs I heard in solitude, some were published over thirty years ago. Since then many of my gleaning have been used by different composers and the musical message sent far and wide.

With the Indian, words hold a secondary or an unimportant place in a song. The music and accompanying action, ceremonial or otherwise, convey the meaning or purpose. When words are used they are few, fragmentary and generally eked out with vocables. Frequently only vocables are attached to a melody. To the Indian, song holds a place similar to that filled for us by wordless instrumental music. In ceremonies, rituals occur that are always rhythmically intoned; each line generally terminates in a refrain. Songs have a place in these rituals, breaking in on the recital particularly when an emotion is evoked, for music is the medium of emotional expression. An old Indian priest explained this peculiarity by saying: " Harmonious sounds unite the people."

Unaccustomed as we are to the use of songs that have no words, we would not only find it difficult to understand their meaning but we would lose much pleasure when singing them. To obviate the perplexities arising from the Indian's peculiar treatment of words and to make clear the meaning of a song, words have been supplied. These words are in no instance a literal translation, for the few broken words that belong to some of the melodies used in these Dances and Games, because of their fragmentary character, would have no value as an interpretation either of the music or of the action. In a number of instances the original vocables are retained, where the music is merely a rhythmical accompaniment to a simple, easily understood movement. Where words are given to a song, they follow closely both the accents and the rhythm of the music. The written stanzas are not meant to be read but to be sung. They express the thought or the feeling that gave rise to the music, they aim to make its meaning understood so that the song can be intelligently sung. In arranging these words, care has been taken never to forget or to change the natural and the psychical environment that belongs to the melody.

Indian songs are very short. They have no preliminary measures, but at once voice the actuating emotion; that done, they come to a close. Although they are so short, they have form and in their structure follow in simple lines the rules of phrasing and motivization taught in our schools. These songs, speaking in general terms, partake more of the character of motifs than of musical compositions. They do not stand alone or apart from the ceremonials or pleasures of which they form an essential feature.

## THE DANCE

The different Indian tribes vary in their modes of dancing; moreover, the same theme is not interpreted by all the tribes in the same manner. In some sections of our country the dancers wear costumes and masks that are symbolic, both in color and form; in other regions, feathers are the principal and emblematic decoration; elsewhere, the men may dance very nearly nude. However diverse the dancing regalia may be or how marked its absence, the Indian dance always presents two characteristics, namely: Dramatic Action and Rhythmic Precision.

Every Indian dance has a meaning. The dance is generally either the acting out of some mythic story or a presentation of a personal experience. Every movement of the body, arms, hands, feet and head is always in strict time with the songs that invariably accompany the dance. Indian dances are complex rather than simple. Their "spontaneous activity" is not the result of "a dominating emotion" but of a desire to present dramatically certain mental pictures. This is particularly true of dances which form a part of religious ceremonials. As a consequence, none of these dances are improvised. All follow forms that have been handed down through generations and have become more or less conventionalized.

When the dance portrays a personal experience the dancer is allowed a freedom of invention not elsewhere permitted. Even in this case the dancer is obliged to follow certain conventional forms, as in the sign language; otherwise his story would not be understood.

On the eastern continent the peoples from whom we are descended had songs and dances peculiar to their different vocations, so on this western continent the song and dance were the accompaniment of the Native industries.

A study of the Indian dramatic dances shows that by means of them the vocations of men and women were lifted out of drudgery, made types of activity and allied to the forces recognized in the religious beliefs of the people. The dances here given, those relative to the Corn and also the Héde-wache, not only illustrate what has been said above but they reflect back a light upon the religious dances that obtained among the eastern nations of antiquity.

When the Indian dances, he dances with freedom; his whole body becomes expressive of the actuating emotion of the scene he intends to portray.  Because of his freedom, his remarkable sense of rhythm and the strong mental picture he aims to present, whether it be the flight of the eagle, the sportive pleasure of birds, the movements of animals, the alertness of the warrior in attack, or in eluding a blow, his motions are always sharply vivid and natural.

It is a pleasure to be able to offer in the following pages a number of Indian songs with their original accompaniment of action, as the two complement each other for the expression of certain native thoughts and aspirations.

Whoever takes part in the dances here presented should never attempt to imitate what is supposed to be the Indian's manner of singing or his dancing steps and postures; in either case the result would probably be an unmeaning burlesque.  Each dancer should have a clear mental picture of the scene to be enacted and then give free play to bodily movements for its expression, always keeping in rhythm with the song, so as to make sound and motion a rhythmic unit.

## THE LIFE OF THE CORN

A DRAMA
IN
FIVE DANCES

INTRODUCTION. — These Dances in their purport and music are taken from the sacred rituals of the Omaha, the Osage and the Pawnee tribes. The richness and beauty of symbolism in the original language suffer a loss of native naïveté in their English interpretation.

The American food plant known by the general term "Corn" was developed ages ago from certain native grasses. The *Euchlaena luxurians* found in Guatemala is probably an ancestor of the maize. The word "maize" belongs to the language of a people living by the Caribbean Sea and never was a universal term for corn among the Indians of our country. The tribes to which maize was known gave it a name derived from their own languages. So very many centuries have passed since corn was a grass that there is no way now of finding out when in the remote past the natives of this continent began the task of developing from a grass a staple article of food like the corn. The process required years of careful observation, manipulation and culture. Not only did the Indians accomplish this task but they took the plant from its tropical surroundings and acclimated it throughout the region east of the Rocky Mountains up to the country of short summers in the North; Cartier, in 1534, found it growing where the city of Montreal now stands.

From this hasty glance at the long history of the maize we can discern the natural sequence of its close relation to the thought and to the life of the Indian, and to a degree understand the love and the reverence with which the corn was held and regarded as a gift from God. Every stage of its growth was ceremonially observed and mentioned in rituals and songs.

Among the Omaha tribe when the time came for planting, four kernels from a red ear of corn were given to each family by the keeper of this sacred rite.  These four red kernels were mixed with the ordinary seed corn, that it might be vivified by them and made to yield an ample harvest.  Red is the symbolic color of life.  In this ceremony is preserved a trace of the far-away time when all the precious seed corn was in the care of priestly keepers.  The ceremony of giving out the four red kernels served to turn the thoughts of the people from a dependence solely on their own labor in cultivating corn to the life-giving power of Wakon'da dwelling within the maize.

In the Omaha Ritual Song of twenty-six stanzas which preceded the distribution of the four red kernels, the Corn speaks.  It tells of its roots reaching in the four directions (where dwell the messengers that bring life), of the growth of its jointed stalk, of the unfolding of its leaves, of the changing color of the silk and of the tassel, of the ripening of the fruit, of the bidding of the people to come, to pluck and to eat.

The music of this Ritual Song is simple.  It is here given with a very brief paraphrase of the words of the Ritual Song.

## Dance I

Introductory Note.—This ceremonial dance touches upon the mystery of the giving of life that life may be maintained; an exchange that links together the different forms of life and enhances the joy of living.

*Properties.* — Thin green mantles; yellow plumes like the corn tassel; bone clips; as many of these articles as there are dancers.

*Directions.* — This dance belongs to both sexes and a number of each should take part, if that is possible. Should there be trees near the open space where the dance takes place, one-half of the dancers, closely wrapped in their green mantles, should be grouped at one side among the trees and the other half similarly placed at the other side. In the center of the space a single dancer stands facing the rear, wrapped about the head and body with the green mantle, leaving only the face exposed.

All being in readiness, the central figure turns slowly, lifts a draped arm and says slowly and impressively:

"Harken! The Corn speaks!"

The group of dancers on the right then sing softly the *first* line only of the Ritual Song in which the Corn speaks. The group of dancers on the left repeat the *same* line like an echo of the first group. Both groups of dancers now begin to move slowly and in rhythm with the following song toward the figure standing in the center of the space, singing, as they move, the Ritual Song *from the beginning:*

### Ritual Song No. 1

Fourfold deep lie my roots within the land;
Clad in green, bearing fruit, Lo! here I stand!
Pluck and eat, life for life, behold, I give!
Shout with joy, dance and sing with all that live.

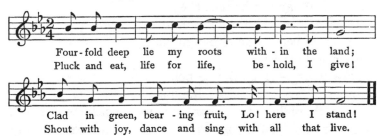

Four-fold deep lie my roots with-in the land;
Pluck and eat, life for life, be-hold, I give!

Clad in green, bear-ing fruit, Lo! here I stand!
Shout with joy, dance and sing with all that live.

At the words "Lo! here I stand!" the company of
dancers should all be standing in a semi-circle.   As the
words in the third line, "Behold, I give!" are sung, the
draped arms should be slightly extended forward as in a
presentation.   The fourth line requires some dramatic
action, but it should be restrained rather than free.   The
arms, still draped with the green mantles, should be
raised a little as the words "Shout with joy" are sung,
and during the singing of the remainder of the line
swayed from side to side in rhythm with the song, always
with a reserve in the movements, because of the mystery
mentioned in the words of the song, that life is maintained by the giving of life.   A pause of about two beats
should follow this Ritual Song.

As "Ho-o! Ho-o!" the opening of the next song, is given,
every dancer should suddenly turn half-way round, give
a movement of the head such as would cause the mantle
to fall back and leave the head with the corn tassel

exposed; the ends of the mantle should be gathered in the hands so that the mantle can wave with the dance as the following song is sung:

### Song No. 2

Ho-o!  Ho-o!
Dance we singing,
Promise bringing
Of the wealth of summer fair;
Hearts beat lightly,
Skies shine brightly,
Youth and Hope are ev'rywhere.

*Refrain:*          Ho-o!  Ho-o!  Ho!  Ho!  Ho!

Ho - o! Ho - o! Dance we sing - ing,

Prom - ise bring - ing Of the wealth

of sum - mer fair; Hearts beat light - ly,

Skies shine bright - ly, Youth and Hope

are ev - 'ry - where. Ho - o,

Ho - o, Ho! Ho! Ho!

As each " Ho-o!" of the refrain is sung, the dancers
should whirl like merry sprites, twine and untwine their
green mantles about their forms until the song begins
again.    Then they should all skip off with springing,
rhythmic steps in open Indian file, letting their mantles
float and wave about them as they wind in and out over
the camp ground carrying "Youth and Hope ev'rywhere."    Every time the refrain is reached, the dancers
should stop and whirl, then as the song begins again
move off in line, dancing as before.    When they are ready
to stop (that can only be done during the singing and
whirling of the refrain), each dancer should whirl from
the line and keep up that movement, singing "Ho!"
until his or her tent is reached.

## DANCE II

INTRODUCTORY NOTE. — The rituals and ceremonies from which this dramatic dance with its accompanying songs are taken have been handed down through numberless generations. They deal with the perpetuation of the vocations of the people and also with the duties of the warrior, who must so protect the people that these vocations can be pursued in peace and safety. The portion of the ritual that relates to the planting of the maize is here given. It is practical in character. The ground is to be cleared of the débris of winter's storms and the dead leaves and twigs gathered into heaps and consumed by fire. When the brown earth is uncovered on the sunny slope it is to be mellowed and made into little hills with flattened tops to receive the kernels of the corn. The first seven of these hills must be ceremonially planted. Into the first hill one kernel of corn is dropped, two kernels are put into the second hill, three in the third, and so on to the seventh, in which are placed seven kernels. The product of these seven little hills must be kept separate, for it is to constitute the "first fruit offering" made to Wakon'da, through the priest, in recognition of the gift of corn as food. After the seven hills are completed, then the rest of the field is similarly prepared and planted. When the kernels are put in the loosened ground they are covered and stamped with the foot, so that each little hill bears the mark, the footprint, of the planter. The Ritual Song depicts the task of planting to its completion and compares the rows of little brown hills to lines of buffalo following one another down the slope. With this vision, suggesting the promise of abundant food, the workers joyfully turn toward the home fireside.

The words given for the first song are a brief paraphrase of the many stanzas of the original Ritual Song, which so touches the necessary acts of the planter as to lift them above a merely prosaic level.

*Properties.* — As this dance represents work, no scarfs or mantles are used. The garments should be plain and the arms free for the necessary dramatic motions in portraying the various acts connected with clearing, preparing and planting the ground. In ancient times the hoe used for this work was made from the shoulder blade of the elk, or a stick three or four feet long shaped at one end like a wedge. Similarly shaped sticks of wood should be used in this dance, one for each dancer. Pouches are required made of brown cloth, with broad bands or straps long enough to pass over the shoulder and chest and to let the pouches hang at the back. Both pouches and straps should be ornamented with geometric designs painted in red, yellow, blue or green; two or three of these colors should be combined in each design. The corn carried within the pouches can be represented by rounded chips, little stones or, when possible, by the corn kernels themselves.

The boys must wear head-bands, carry bows and have quivers hung at their backs. They must scatter around the border of the "field," move watchfully about, peer into the distance and act as if on the alert to detect or to meet any prowling enemy.

*Directions.* — A space should be set apart to represent the "field" where the dramatic action takes place. This dance requires considerable dramatic pantomime. The words in the two lines of each stanza of the song serve as a prelude to the action which follows. Sometimes the action may be confined to the refrain, but generally there must be acting throughout the singing both of the words and the refrain. Much in this dance must be left to the imagination and skill of the group of dancers, who should rehearse together and decide how best to make a clear, strong picture. The native music here given belongs to the act of preparing the ground and planting the kernels of corn. Attention is called to the second, fourth, sixth and eighth measures of the song. The three-quarter notes and the eighth and rest should be accented by movements of the hoe, the foot or both. The rhythm of the first measure is a little different from that of the third, fifth and seventh, caused by the third note being a quarter note, denoting a definite act or pause; the remaining four notes of the first measure are flowing, as well as all the notes of the third, fifth and seventh measures. By observing these little points in the music the drama will be given variety and made more picturesque and effective.

At the beginning of the song the dancers should be at a little distance from the space set apart to represent the "field," so that they will be able at the proper time to go toward it. As the first line of the first stanza is sung the dancers should stand in a loose group, adjust their hoes and pouches to be ready to go to the "field"; during the singing of the second line they should break into a file and move off. All these movements of body, hands and feet must be in strict time and rhythm with the music.

## Song No. 1

### I

Here we stand ready now to go on our way
To the field, buried under leaves dead and gray.
> *Refrain:*    Ah hey they,
> Ah hey hey they,
> Ah hey they ha!
> Ah hey they,
> Ah hey hey they,
> Ah hey they ha!

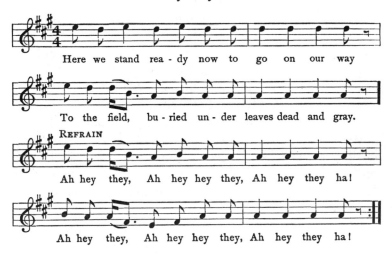

Here we stand rea - dy now to go on our way

To the field, bu - ried un - der leaves dead and gray.

REFRAIN

Ah hey they, Ah hey hey they, Ah hey they ha!

Ah hey they, Ah hey hey they, Ah hey they ha!

By the end of the first line of the refrain the dancers
will have reached the "field" and have begun to dispose
themselves over the space. Seven must stand in the
first row, where they are to make the seven ceremonial
hills. These seven dancers should lead the motions of
all the others, so that the movements may present even
lines, as in the bowing of violins in an orchestra. The

refrain should be repeated as many times as is necessary while the dancers are taking position, clearing the field, etc. The number of repeats must be determined upon at the rehearsals of the dancers. Sufficient time should be taken to bring out the picture and to give it in perfect rhythm with the music. When the refrain closes, the dead leaves and twigs are supposed to be gathered into heaps ready to be burned.

### 2

See the fire send its "word of flame" mounting high,
Now the smoke rolls about the earth, shuts out sky.
*Refrain:*    Ah hey they,
Ah hey hey they,
Ah hey they ha!
Ah hey they,
Ah hey hey they,
Ah hey they ha!

The action for this stanza should indicate the heat of the fire; shielding the face, pushing back stray leaves or twigs to the burning heap; the rolling smoke follows the dancers, who here and there try to escape it. This scene will require study to bring out the picture rhythmically. It should form a contrast to the preceding and the following scene, in both of which the movements are more or less uniform. In this scene groups should emphasize certain conditions: the fire, the smoke, the work of keeping the heaps together, so that the picture will be one of action diverse to a degree and yet every movement dominated by the rhythm of the song; the picture will thus be made a unit.

### 3

Mellow earth, make the little hills smooth on top,
On the earth softly the kernels we drop.

> *Refrain:*      Ah hey they,
> Ah hey hey they,
> Ah hey they ha!
> Ah hey they,
> Ah hey hey they,
> Ah hey they ha!

In the action of this stanza the seven dancers in the front row make seven ceremonial hills, mellowing the earth with the wooden hoes and gathering it into little hills made smooth on top.  The pouches are swung to the front, the corn taken out with one hand while the other holds the hoe at rest, and the kernels are dropped on the softened earth.  The dancers should be careful to remember that in the ceremonial row of seven hills but one kernel is to be dropped in the first hill, two in the second, and so on up to seven in the seventh hill.  All the dancers scattered over the "field" must follow the movements of the seven in charge of the seven ceremonial hills.

### 4

Cover all gently, leave the print of our feet
On the earth mellowed fine, so brown, so sweet.

> *Refrain:*      Ah hey they,
> Ah hey hey they,
> Ah hey they ha!
> Ah hey they,
> Ah hey hey they,
> Ah hey they ha!

In the action for this stanza the hoe and the feet of

the dancers have a special part. The movements of the dancers should represent the covering of the dropped seed with the mellowed earth and the making of the footprint on the top of the little hill within which the seed is now hidden. In the native Ritual Song the term "footprint" is used symbolically; it represents a person — in this instance the one who had done the work — also the work itself that has been accomplished. The dancers should be careful to remember the rhythm of the second, fourth, sixth and eighth measures, as these can be used to emphasize "footprints" and also the completion of the task. During a repeat of the refrain the dancers should drop their hoes and gather in groups as if to look at the field; this action will bring them into the position required for the fifth stanza.

5

How like lines of buffalo upon the slope,
Lie our little brown hills, so full now of hope.
*Refrain:*    Ah hey they,
          Ah hey hey they,
          Ah hey they ha!
          Ah hey they,
          Ah hey hey they,
          Ah hey they ha!

The motions of the hands and the movements of the body should indicate that in looking over the field one is struck by the striped appearance made by the rows of little hills, recalling the resemblance to the buffalo descending the slope. The final "ha!" of the refrain should indicate pleasure. A brief silence should follow, during which the dancers pick up their hoes, adjust their pouches, fall into line and sing the following song:

## Song No. 2

Light our hearts and gay
As we homeward take our way,
While the winds about us play,
Singing as we go.
Hy-ya hy-ya hy-ya ho!
Hy-ya hy-ya hy-ya ho!
Hy-ya ho!
Ho!
Hy-ya ho!

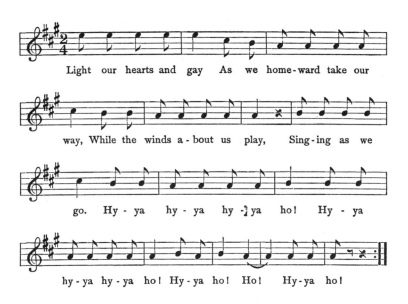

Light our hearts and gay    As    we home-ward take our

way, While the winds a - bout us    play,    Sing-ing as we

go.  Hy - ya    hy - ya    hy -ya    ho!    Hy - ya

hy -ya  hy -ya  ho!  Hy -ya  ho!  Ho!    Hy -ya  ho!

This song should be repeated many times as all the
dancers, with rhythmic, springing steps, wind about the
camp ground before they finally disperse.

## DANCE III

INTRODUCTORY NOTE. — This dance is from the Corn Ritual Song and is a dramatization of a visit to the planted field after the lapse of a few weeks. Life has been stirring in the kernels of corn that had been hidden within the little hills, and the kernels now call to those who had planted them to come and see what was taking place.

*Properties.* — The same as those used in the preceding dance. Both the boys and the girls should wear the same costume as in Dance II.

*Directions.* — The scene should be the same as in Dance II. The "field" to be visited should be in the same place as the space set apart for the "field" where the little hills were made and planted.

A part of the boys should act as guards of the "field" as before. A few should scatter among the girls and join in looking at the sprouting corn as it breaks through the soil, and these should join in singing the song.

At the opening of the dance the dancers should be discovered standing in groups as though they had accidentally met as neighbors of the same village. They should stand at the same place whence they had started to go to the "field" in the preceding dance. The groups should be talking in dumb show. Suddenly each group should act as if its attention had been arrested by a sound, and while in this attitude of arrested attention all should begin to sing the following song:

## Song

### I

A call I hear!
Hark! soft the tones and weak.
Again the call!
Come! our feet that call must seek.

*Refrain:*      Hey hey they,
Ah hey hey they,
Ah hey hey they,
Again the call!
Ah hey hey they,
Ah hey hey they,
Ah hey hey they,
Ah hey they.

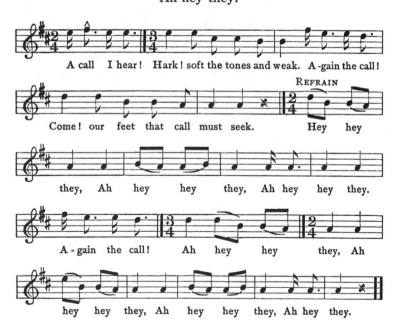

This dramatic dance will require to be rehearsed and the details planned by the dancers, so that a clear picture may be brought out and also the native poetic thought embodied in the Ritual Song from which it is taken. A few hints can be given, but much of the action must depend upon the imagination and dramatic feeling of the dancers.

As the first line, "A call I hear!" is sung some one should raise the hand toward the ear, another raise it as a warning to keep quiet. The line "Hark! soft the tones and weak" is an address to one another in the groups. Then comes another sudden arrest, "Again the call!" These three lines should be sung without any change of position either by the groups or by the individuals. Action should be confined to the hands and the head. When singing the fourth line all should begin to stir, to adjust their pouches, tighten their hold on the wooden hoes and, as if moved by a common impulse, should prepare to go and seek the source of the call. In their going the groups should not fall into one line but each group move by itself. During the refrain the dancers should act as if in doubt which way to go. At the line "Again the call!" all should stop as if arrested, and then move off again when the refrain is taken up. All the groups should keep the rhythm of the music. There should be a good deal of by-play and the action should indicate bewilderment, both as to the meaning of the call and the locality whence it comes. It should appear as though some of the groups are baffled in their attempt to locate the call.

2

A call I hear!
Hark! it is near at hand,
    The call! The call!
Floats to us where we now stand.
*Refrain:*          Hey hey they,
        Ah hey hey they,
        Ah hey hey they,
          Again the call!
        Ah hey hey they,
        Ah hey hey they,
        Ah hey hey they,
        Ah hey they.

The action of this stanza shows the dancers being led
by the call to the "field," where the call seems to become clearer and at last is there located. The dancers
should scatter in groups, while different individuals
should look about searchingly but without breaking the
groups. These should move here and there seeking for
the "footprints" that had been left on the smooth tops
of the little hills, and so lead to the action required for
the next stanza. Whenever in the song the line "The
call! The call!" occurs, there should be an apparent
arrest of movement among the dancers as if to listen.

3

Again the call!
Forth to the light of day
    They come! They come!
Come pushing upward their way.
*Refrain:*          Hey hey they,
        Ah hey hey they,
        Ah hey hey they,

They call! They come!
Ah hey hey they,
Ah hey hey they,
Ah hey hey they,
Ah hey they.

"Day" is the symbol of life; the kernels are coming "into the light of day" in the original Ritual Song, meaning they are entering into life. They call as they come, struggling and pushing their way through the breaking earth. This life movement should be indicated by the motions of the dancers as they pass in groups with rhythmic steps from one little hill to another. Directions as to how these motions should be made would hardly be helpful; the dancers can best plan this pantomime.

### 4
Again the call!
Two feeble leaves are seen,
They call! They call!
Soon shall we stand clad with green!
*Refrain:*        Hey hey they,
Ah hey hey they,
Ah hey hey they,
They call! They call!
Ah hey hey they,
Ah hey hey they,
Ah hey hey they,
Ah hey they.

The original Ritual Song tells that the feeble leaves, the first shoots, cannot stand or support themselves; they are helpless as infants. But they have come to the "light of day," "have entered into life," and they will grow, become strong and stand, stretching ever higher into the light. The native stanzas portray the progressive movements of the corn from feeble helplessness into the power of life. The action of the dancers should convey this meaning by appropriate pantomime.

5

They call! They call!
Up springs our jointed stem,
They call! They call!
Golden fruit shall grow on them.

*Refrain:*      Hey hey they,
            Ah hey hey they,
            Ah hey hey they,
                They call! They call!
            Ah hey hey they,
            Ah hey hey they,
            Ah hey hey they,
            Ah hey they.

In this stanza the promise of fruit is given. The dancers should show excitement not only at the wonderful spectacle they observe but because of the promise given.

They should still keep in groups as they move about and exult in the results that have come from the little hills where they left their "footprints."

In the original Ritual Song there are more than a score of stanzas in which the various occurrences of the growth of the corn are mentioned, mingled with symbolic imagery. "Footprints" represent both labor and ownership. Those who planted the kernels look

for these marks and rejoice over what they find.    They
had begun their planting "like a game," a venture;
whether it would be successful or not no one could
tell.    But success had come.    The action for the last
stanza should indicate an abandonment to delight; hoes
should be dropped as the  groups mingle and  act out
pleasure not only at what is seen but what is promised.

A pause should follow, then the hoes should be picked
up and the dancers gather by twos and threes in a line
to return home;  as they start they break into the same
song which they sang on the return from making and
planting the little hills:

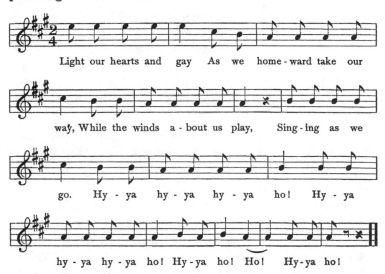

Light our hearts and    gay    As    we    home - ward take    our
way, While the winds a - bout us play,    Sing - ing    as    we
go.    Hy - ya    hy - ya    hy - ya    ho!    Hy - ya
hy - ya    hy - ya    ho!    Hy - ya    ho!    Ho!    Hy - ya    ho!

The dancers should keep up the song and rhythmic
dance until their individual tents are reached.

## Dance IV

Introductory Note. — This dance, taken from the Corn Ritual, represents a visit to the field later in the season when the harvest time is near at hand. The keynote of this visit is in a line of one of the many stanzas of the original Ritual Song, "I go in readiness of mind." The mind is assured, prepared to find in the place where the "footprints" had been made, where the little kernels had broken the covering of earth to reach "the light of day," that these have now grown tall and strong under the summer sun and are "standing in the fulness of day." This assurance is justified, for the corn is found ready to pluck, and some of its ears are joyously carried to the people at home.

*Properties.* — The same costumes as those worn by the boys and girls in Dance II and III. The green scarfs used in Dance I will be needed in the latter part of this dance; these can be folded and carried in the pouches and pockets.

*Directions.* — The scene should be laid in the same place as the two preceding dances and the dancers should gather at the same spot whence they started to the "field" in Dance II and III.

The dancers, both boys and girls, should be discovered standing in an open group talking together in dumb show, evidently discussing the probabilities as to the ripening of the corn. They may have been saying: "Already the boys are shouting, The cattail is in bloom!" This was a sign that the time had come for the corn to be ripe. Some one whose mind was "in readiness" makes the suggestion (in pantomime) to go to the "field"; to this all agree, and the group breaks into lines as the boy and girl dancers sing the following song:

## Song

### I

In readiness of mind to the field we go,
Where we footprints made, there stately
        jointed stalks grow.
Loud rustle the long leaves, bright the tassels
        wave o'er each row.

*Refrain:*      Ah hey hey hey they,
         Ah hey hey they,
         Ah hey hey hey they,
         Ah hey hey they,
         Ah hey they.

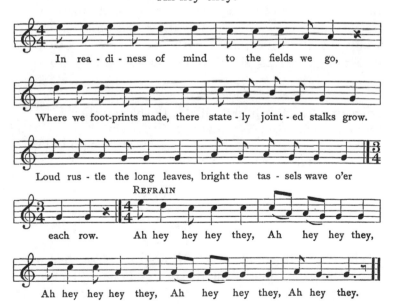

The steps of the dancers must be in rhythm with the song and all movements should indicate a feeling of assurance. When the "field" is reached certain motions of the feet should suggest a memory of the "footprints." The "field" is now covered by rows of tall cornstalks; therefore, when the "field" is reached the dancers should move in parallel lines, as if they were passing between these rows. Some lines should cross at right angles, giving the effect of walking between high barriers, along pathways that intersect each other at right angles. When the dancers pass along these alleys, so to speak, movements should be made to indicate brushing against or pushing out of the way the "long rustling leaves" of the corn, and to point to the "waving tassels" far above their heads. This pantomime, with its rhythmic movements suggesting long lines of cornstalks, the brushing aside with the hands of the long leaves of the stalks, should make an effective picture.

2

Strongly the ears shoot out, fill'd with golden grain,
Up into the full light, life flowing in each vein,
Sacred the corn now stands ready to give its strength full fain.

*Refrain:*      Ah hey hey hey they,
                Ah hey hey they,
                Ah hey hey hey they,
                Ah hey hey they,
                Ah hey they.

The length of the original Ritual Song, together with the picturesque quality of the native language, permits the bringing out in full detail of this scene of the cornfield:

the ears standing at angles from the stalk, and the husks full of kernels replete with life-giving power. Because of this power the corn has now "become sacred," filled with life from Wakon'da, thereby related to that great power and through it linked to the life of mankind. The idea of this unity throughout all nature, including man, is fundamental to Indian thought and belief. It is expressed in all his religious ceremonies and also in his vocations, both serious and playful. In the present instance it appeals to him through the planting, the growth, the maturing and the use of the corn, giving its life to man.

To convey the picture of the cornfield, and to suggest the thoughts that imbue the scene as expressed in the native rituals, will require some study, but the effort will be well worth while. These thoughts were vital upon this continent centuries before the land became our home. The maize in all its richness and beauty has become ours to enjoy, and while we accept this gift let us not fail to catch and to hold the lingering vibrations of its native teaching that aimed to lift the thoughts of the worker in the cornfield to the Great Giver of Life and Beauty.

In planning the pantomime for this stanza the dancers should not forget the rhythm of the song and to keep the lines as though they were walking between rows of tall cornstalks.

3

Where'er we look wide fields wait harvest to meet;
Ripe are the ears we pluck, juicy the corn we eat;
Filling our arms, we go homeward, happy hearts there we meet.
  *Refrain:*  Ah hey hey hey they,
      Ah hey hey they,
      Ah hey hey hey they,
      Ah hey hey they,
      Ah hey they.

The action requisite for the interpretation of this stanza by pantomime is comparatively easy, as looking over the field ready for harvest, and plucking a few ears of the corn. Care should be taken not to appear to touch the row where the seven hills were made, for the product of these are to be used as the "first-fruit offering." During the singing of the first line of the third stanza a few of the dancers should slip behind some of the others and there take out their scarfs from the pouches or pockets, make each scarf into a loose bundle and carry it upon the folded arms as though it was filled with ears of corn. In this way, a few at a time, the dancers can secure their scarfs, and arrange them to look like bundles of corn to be taken homeward.

All the lines that have been moving as between rows of corn should now come together and form a long line and with dancing, rhythmic steps, and arms filled with corn, return to the starting place, and from there wind about the camp ground singing the refrain, which can be repeated *ad lib.* until they finally disperse and go to their tents.

## DANCE V

INTRODUCTORY NOTE. — This dance represents the bringing of the "first-fruit offering" of the corn from the seven little hills that were ceremonially planted after the dead leaves of winter had been cleared away. The dancers who follow the seven leaders carrying the corn-stalks represent the people in triumphal procession in honor of Corn as "Mother breathing forth life." Both words and music of the song for this procession are taken from a great religious ceremony of the Pawnee wherein Corn is spoken of as A-ti-ra, Mother, with the prefix H' signifying breath, the sign of life. "H'A-ti-ra" ("Mother breathing forth life") is repeated over and over and is the only word used in this song. The repetition is not an idle procedure but an awakening of echoes in the native mind, of all that Corn has meant to his ancestors and race during the centuries. The repeated words imply contemplation on the subject. This song when heard sung by a hundred or more could not fail to impress one with its majestic fervor. The beautiful, bountiful maize giving its life that others might enjoy life, on another plane, is here reverently and joyously proclaimed "Mother."

*Properties.* — Green and other bright colored scarfs or mantles, as many as there are dancers, boys and girls, also wreaths made of long leaves like those of the corn-stalk; these can be manufactured from green paper. Tall yellow plumes, similar to the tassel of the corn, and fastened to the wreath in such manner that when the wreath is worn the plume will stand above the forehead.

Seven cornstalks, or wands so wound with green as to appear like the stalk of the corn with its tassel.

*Directions.* — All the dancers should be wrapped in their mantles and have on their wreaths, the erect tassel plume standing directly over the middle of the forehead. Boys and girls must mingle in this dance. All dress as before, with the addition of the mantles. Implements, pouches and bows and arrows are not used. Of the seven who are to lead, four should be boys and three girls. When leading the procession and carrying the cornstalks, the first line of four should be a boy, two girls, a boy; the second line of three should be a boy, a girl, a boy. These seven must wear green robes or mantles and hold the cornstalks, with their hands draped by the mantle. The other dancers can wear green or other colored mantles or scarfs. The boys must sing the songs, for the volume of sound must be full in order to produce the true effect of this impressive ceremony. The seven dancers who have been selected to act as leaders should stand in a group by themselves in front of the other dancers, who are in loose groups at the rear. On the space which heretofore in these dances has represented the "field," the seven cornstalks or wands should be laid in a windrow on the ground. When ready to begin the dance the dancers should be discovered in the two groups as already described, talking quietly in dumb show.

The seven leaders, who are in the front group by themselves, appear to consult together; then, led by one of their number, sing the following song:

## Song No. 1

### I

Golden on ev'ry hand,
Waving, the cornfields stand,
    Calling us thither;
    Calling us thither,
First-fruits to cull and bring
Our sacred offering
    To great Wakon'da,
        Giver of Corn.

Gold - en  on  ev - 'ry  hand, Wav - ing,  the corn - fields stand,

Call - ing  us  thi - ther; Call - ing  us  thi - ther,

First - fruits  to  cull  and  bring Our  sa - cred  of - fer - ing

To  great  Wa - kon' - da,  Giv - er  of  Corn.

During the singing the seven leaders stand together wrapped in their green mantles. All the other dancers are grouped at a little distance back, still talking as at first in dumb show. At the third line they stop talking, at the fourth line they give attention to the seven leaders, at the fifth line they join in the song. During the singing of this stanza there should be no change in the relative positions of the two groups, but during the singing all who sing should keep up a gentle rhythmic swaying of the body.

2

Now to the field we hie,
Where stands the corn so high,
Calling us thither;
Calling us thither,
First-fruits to cull and bring
Our sacred offering
To great Wakon'da,
Giver of Corn.

The seven leaders, at the beginning of the first line of the second stanza, slowly fall into line and with deliberate rhythmic steps move toward the "field," reaching it by the fifth line, and while singing that line they should pick up the cornstalks and hold them, with their hands draped with their green mantles, high to the front.

At the close of the first stanza the other group of dancers should resume a dumb show of speaking to one another until the third line of the second stanza, when they change their attitude and give attention; at the fourth line they join in the song, and at the fifth move toward the "field" where are the seven leaders. By the close of the second stanza all the dancers should be in one group at the "field."

All the dancers stand there at the "field" a moment in silence. Then the seven leaders sing the introduction to the following Processional Song:

Song No. 2

*Introduction:*    Follow Mother Corn,
Who breathes forth life!

*Chorus:*    H'A-ti-ra, H'A-ti-ra, H'A-ti-ra, A-ti-ra,
H'A-ti-ra, A-ti-ra, H'A-ti-ra, A-ti-ra,
A-ti-ra, H'A-ti-ra, A-ti-ra.

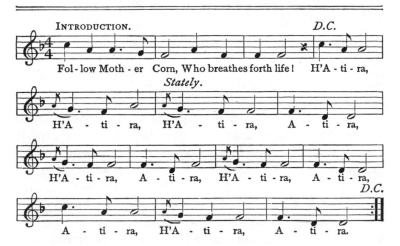

Fol-low Moth-er Corn, Who breathes forth life! H'A-ti-ra, H'A-ti-ra, H'A-ti-ra, A-ti-ra, H'A-ti-ra, A-ti-ra, H'A-ti-ra, A-ti-ra, A-ti-ra, H'A-ti-ra, A-ti-ra.

This song is retained as sung in the original Pawnee ceremony; the meaning has already been explained.

The introduction is sung by the seven leaders, who advance in two rows, four in the first, three in the second, and in this manner they lead the Processional Dance. At the chorus all the other dancers fall in behind the leaders, either in couples or singly, every one singing. All steps must be rhythmic and in time with the music. The seven leaders move steadily, also in time with the music, as they hold the cornstalks high, while the followers wave their scarfs or mantles and dance happily and lightly, but with dignity. The picture should be one of contrast as the procession takes its way among trees and through the sunny fields, the seven moving evenly, with the corn held high, and the joyous, fluttering group of dancers following.

The Life of the Corn culminates in a delight of color, movement and song.

## CALLING THE FLOWERS

INTRODUCTORY NOTE. — This dance is derived from a ceremony, observed among the Indians of the North Pacific Coast, in which the spirits dwelling beneath the ground are called to come and join those who are dancing. The dancer who calls the spirits moves with gliding steps, the arms outstretched, the hands beckoning upward in a gentle, enticing manner. The grace, dignity and earnestness of this dance linger with the writer as a beautiful memory after the lapse of many years.

*Properties.* — A green scarf for the Caller. Blue, white and rosy scarfs for as many dancers as will personate the three Flowers that respond to the call: Violets, Wild-roses and Daisies. A twisted rope of green to link the dancing Flowers together in the final dance.

*Directions.* — A clear space will be required large enough for all the dancers to move about in the final dance. Those who personate the Flowers should be hidden from view until the time when they are to respond to the call. In the properties enumerated above, mention is made only of scarfs. The picturesqueness of the dance would be enhanced if the dancers wore headdresses shaped somewhat like the flowers and made of appropriate colored paper; blue or lilac for the Violets, with a touch of yellow; deep pink or pale red for the Wild-roses, with a little yellow for the stamens; white with yellow for the Daisies. The twisted rope of green paper should be made over heavy twine, so as to be strong enough for the dancers to grasp in the final dance. All these decorative articles should be made in the camp.

The dancer who acts as the Caller should wear the green scarf loosely thrown about the head and body. If the voice of this dancer is not strong enough to be clearly heard by those who look on at a little distance, then two other persons should stand one at each side of the open space and sing with the dancer who is the Caller. These two extra singers should be wrapped in green scarfs and stand quietly as interested spectators while the dancer calls. Care should be taken to give the words of the songs with clearness and distinctness, so that every person within hearing distance can catch them easily.

## The Dance

The scene opens with the one who is to call the Flowers standing in the center, looking about in different directions. Suddenly, as if the thought occurred to call for companions, the following song is begun:

### Song No. 1

#### CALL TO THE FLOWERS

Hither come, come to me, flowers!
   Wake from your sleep.
Oh, hither come, hither come, flowers!
   Hear me calling,
   Wake from your sleep, O flowers!
   Hark! some one comes.

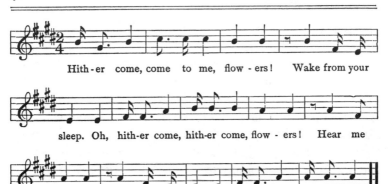

Hith-er come, come to me, flow-ers! Wake from your

sleep. Oh, hith-er come, hith-er come, flow - ers! Hear me

call-ing, Wake from your sleep, O flowers! Hark! some one comes!

With the song, movement begins. The steps taken should be gentle and gliding, the arms outstretched as in entreaty, the hands moved as in beckoning, not with one finger but all the fingers slowly bending toward the open palm. The dancer should think what the action means as she glides about the open space, and strive to carry out the picture of awakening the sleeping flowers, of bidding them to "come hither." It is possible that more time may be required by some dancers to produce the picture than merely singing the song once through would give; in that case, that portion of the song having the words "Hear me calling, Wake from your sleep, O flowers!" can be repeated once or twice, to meet the requirements of the dancer. The last line, "Hark! some one comes!" should be given with dramatic action.

These words are the cue for those who are to represent the Violets to prepare to enter from different points on the right, and to make a soft, stirring sound before they come into view, singing the following song:

## Song No. 2

### SONG OF THE VIOLETS

Violets have come in heav'nly hue;
With fragrance sweet they bring to you
Love from the dell where they grew
Close to the earth so true.

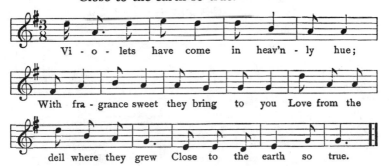

Vi - o - lets have come in heav'n - ly hue;

With fra - grance sweet they bring to you Love from the

dell where they grew Close to the earth so true.

The Violets dance with quiet steps in rhythm with the song. They slowly advance and gather in a loose circle about the Caller, whom, as they come near, each one lightly touches, to give "Love from the dell where they grew." Then they retire to the edge of the open space at the right and sit on the ground in little groups. When they are quiet and in their places, the Caller moves toward them, then turns, stops, looks at the empty side at the left and sings:

## Song No. 1

### CALL TO THE FLOWERS

[See page 42]

The last line gives the cue to those who represent the Wild-roses to make a rustling sound where they are hidden on the left. They enter with light springing steps, singing:

## Song No. 3

### SONG OF THE WILD-ROSES

Wild-roses come all bright and gay,
Blushing red like dawn of day;
Dancing come they, full of play,
Hiding all their thorns away.
Wild-roses come all bright and gay,
Blushing red like dawn of day,
Dancing come they, full of play.

The Wild-roses dance about gaily; they circle the quiet little clumps of Violets that remain seated. The

Wild-roses frolic around the Caller, capering about in wild freedom but keeping their steps in exact time with their song.   Finally they pause in groups at the left.

After a moment, the Caller moves toward the rear of the open space and while there once again sings:

### Song No. 1
#### CALL TO THE FLOWERS
[ See page 42 ]

At the close of the song the dancers who are to represent the Daisies give a trilling shout and appear from the rear of the open space, skipping; their leader holds the end of a long green rope, which is caught hold of by each dancer who follows, all singing:

### Song No. 4
#### SONG OF THE DAISIES

Up from meadows free,
Coming full of glee,
Troop the Daisies white,
Dancing in the light,
All skipping blithe and gay.
Now we make a chain,
Singing as we twine
Then back into line —
Merry at play!

Up from mead-ows free, Com - ing full of glee,

Troop the Dai - sies white, Danc - ing in the light,

All skip - ping blithe and gay.

Now we make a chain, Sing - ing as we twine,

Then back in - to line— Mer - ry at play!

As the Daisies skip in the open space, the dancers are widely separated as they hold on to the rope; at the words "Now we make a chain" the Violets, who had risen as the Daisies entered, move toward the string of dancers; the Wild-roses also come toward the chain and grasp the green rope. The colors of the flowers should alternate and all the Flowers should have hold of the rope and cling to it as to a great green stem. Then all circle around the Caller, who is the last to grasp the stem. As all the Flowers dance they repeat Song No. 4, beginning at the words "Troop the Daisies white," etc.

This chain of flowers should make, as they dance, interweaving figures.  These can be left to the fancy of the dancers, but just what they are to be must be decided upon beforehand and rehearsed; otherwise the dance will not be successful and pleasing.

The dances for each kind of flower will require practice, for the character of each flower should be well brought out; the gentleness of the Violets can make a charming contrast to the waywardness of the Wild-roses and the pliant Daisies who are at home everywhere.

## APPEAL FOR CLEAR SKY

INTRODUCTORY NOTE. — Among those Indian tribes that lived outside the semi-arid sections of our country, the storm with its destructive force was the representative of war, and thunder was a war god.

Warfare was widespread among the tribes dwelling in the Mississippi valley; yet among these people the desirability and value of peace were recognized. Honors won in a defensive fight gave the warrior higher rank than those gained in wars of aggression. Rituals belonging to religious ceremonies, and also to war rites, taught that the first duty of the warrior was to protect the women and children, the fields and the food supply, for his strong arm and ready courage made the tribe's only wall of defence against enemies.

These tribes had ceremonies relating to the maintenance of peace not only within the tribe but for the purpose of forming peaceful relations with other tribes. The clear sky was the symbol of peace, of happiness and of prosperity, conditions the very opposite of those that attended war.

When a peace ceremony was in progress, if a storm arose it was looked upon as an omen of disaster. At such a time, when clouds gathered, the people joined in ceremonial songs and appeals for clear sky, the symbol of peace.

The following dramatic dance and the accompanying songs are employed on such an occasion. The songs are taken from ceremonies used to promote peace.

*Properties.* — Staffs, about three feet long, with small blue flags, as many as there are dancers, the same number of blue head-bands and blue sashes. The latter are to be worn from the right shoulder across the breast and tied at the waist under the left arm. A drum.

*Directions.* — This dance belongs to both sexes and boys and girls should, if possible, join in it.

## THE DANCE

All the dancers stand facing the East, in one or more rows deep, according to the number, their staffs held in the right hand so that the flags will hang in front of each dancer, covering the chest, as they begin the following song:

## Song No. 1

Away, away, dark clouds, away!
Leave the sky!
Go far away, dark clouds, to-day!
Leave the sky!
Stormy clouds, go far away, far away,
Stormy clouds, no longer stay!
Leave the sky!
Go far away, dark clouds, to-day!
Leave the sky!
Stormy clouds, go far way, far away!
Stormy clouds, begone!

A - way,    a - way, dark clouds, a - way! Leave the    sky! Go

far  a - way, dark clouds, to - day! Leave the  sky! Storm-y clouds, go

far  a - way,  far  a - way, Storm - y clouds, no    long - er stay!

Leave    the    sky!    Go    far    a - way,    dark

clouds,    to - day!  Leave the    sky!  Storm - y  clouds, go

*D.C.*

far    a - way,    far    a - way! Storm - y    clouds, be - gone!

## FIRST APPEAL

In the first line at each "away" the dancers should look up toward the East and move a step forward in that direction. At the line "Leave the sky!" they should point their flags toward the East, keeping the staff out on a level with the body, and accent it by thrusting it forward as if pointing to the East, being careful not to change the level of the staff. At the second "Leave the sky!" the level of the staffs must be raised to about the chin of the dancer and the same pointing motion repeated at this level. At the third "Leave the sky!" the staffs are raised to the level of the dancers' eyes and the same pointing movement repeated. At the fourth "Leave the sky!" the level of the staffs is raised to a line with the top of the head and the pointing motions again given. At the last line, "Stormy clouds, begone!" the staffs and flags should be raised aloft and waved with precision to the rhythm of the song. The steps and movements of the body should be that of backward and forward, to give a pulsating effect, all in exact time with the music. The drum should be beaten in ⅜ time, the first and third stroke heavier than the second and fourth. This series of movements constitutes the Appeal to the East.

The dancers next turn to the North, repeat the song and all the movements of staff and body in exactly the same manner.

The dancers now turn toward the West and go through the song and movements without any variation.

They then turn toward the South and repeat song and movements as before. This brings the First Appeal to a close.

## SECOND APPEAL

All the dancers gather in a loose group in the center of the open space, where they divide into two lines that must cross each other at right angles. When this cross-figure is formed, all, as they stand, should face the East. The staffs should be held at an angle similar to that of a baton and then swayed to the rhythm of the following song of pleading and of hope:

## Song No. 2

Come, soft skies of blue,
O'er the earth of verdant hue
Bend in peace!
Clouds by thy sunny breath all are gone,
Blue Sky!
Joy now fills our hearts anew,
Sorrows cease;
Songs of birds sing of thy peace,
Blue Sky!

As the dancers sing they should take a step sidewise to the right, then return to the first position; then a step to the left and return, so that the whole cross-figure has a swaying motion accentuating the rhythm of the song, which should be sung smoothly and flowingly. When the words "Blue Sky!" are sung the flags should be raised aloft and waved in rhythm and then returned to the previous level. The song should be repeated several times and the figure maintained as the singers face the North, West, South and back to the East. Then the dancers should break into groups and, still singing the song and dancing rhythmically, disperse to their tents.

## The Hé-de Wa-chi

### An Omaha Festival of Joy

INTRODUCTORY NOTE. — For centuries the home of the Omaha tribe has been in the region now known as the State of Nebraska, north of the city which bears their name. There they dwelt in permanent villages, surrounded by their garden plots of corn, beans, squashes, etc. From these villages every year in June all the tribes except the sick and infirm went forth to follow the buffalo herds in order to obtain their supply of meat and pelts. As this tribal hunt was essential to the needs of the life of the people, it was a very serious affair, initiated with religious ceremonies and conducted under strict rules enforced by duly appointed officers. It was at the close of this great tribal hunt, when food and clothing had been secured, while Summer lingered and the leaves had not yet begun to fall, so that brightness was still over the land, that this Festival of Joy took place. Like all Indian ceremonies, the Hé-de Wa-chi embodied a teaching that was for the welfare of the tribe, a teaching drawn from nature and dramatically enacted by the people. The Omaha tribe was made up of ten distinct groups, each one having its own name, a set of names for those born within the group, and certain religious symbols and ceremonies committed to its care. By tribal rites and regulations these ten distinct groups were welded together to form the tribe, whose strength and prosperity depended upon internal harmony and unity.

The Hé-de Wa-chi taught the people what this unity really stood for. The central object of the ceremony was a tree, which was the symbol of the tribe; its branches were as the different groups composing the tribe, the twigs that made up the branches were as the individuals that formed the groups.

The Omaha had special ceremonies for the preparation of the central object. They cut a tree, left a tuft of branches at the top and painted the trunk in alternate bands of red and black. The red bands represented day, the black, night; the decoration as a whole stood for the continuity of life. This pole was planted in a broad open space. As the melodious Call to the Ceremony echoed over the land, the people gathered from their tents. Each one of the ten groups took its respective place and all the groups formed a wide circle about the tree. Every one, down to the little children, carried a twig with leaves. These they held aloft as they made their rhythmic, ceremonial approaches to the tree, and afterward danced about the sacred symbol.

It was a wonderful and a beautiful scene that took place on the prairies years ago, when hundreds of Omahas moved to the rhythm of the sacred songs, waving the green sprays as they danced up to the symbolic tree and circled about it with thanksgiving and joy. It was thus they exemplified tribal unity, wherein every one was a part of the living whole.

This ancient American ceremony should live anew with us wherever we gather to enjoy the delights of nature in goodly company.

*Directions.* — It may be difficult to prepare a young

tree for the central pole after the manner of the Omaha; if so, a space around a single tree can be made to serve. Bands of red and black muslin or paper should be put about the tree trunk; these are to symbolize the days and nights enjoyed during the camp life. The members of the camp should be divided into groups and each group have a name and a color. Small branches should be gathered, equal in number to those who will take part in the dance. If actual branches are not available, wands can be used; to these fluttering decorations of green paper should be attached, also a streamer the color of the group. Each group should be assigned a place in the wide circle that is to be made about the tree.

When all are ready the following Call should be sung. The Indian words are retained, as they are easy to pronounce and fit the meaning, and are adapted to the long echoing cadences of the Call.

### Song No. 1

THE CALL

Zha-wa i-ba i-ba e-he,
Zha-wa i-ba i-ba ha e-he.

Zha - wa i - ba    i -    - ba    e - he, . .

Zha - wa i - ba    i - ba ha . .    e - he. . . . . .

[Words: Zha-wa = to rejoice; i-ba = come; ha = vowel prolongation of the syllable ba; e-he = I bid you. "I bid you come to rejoice."]

This English translation of the native words does not convey the stirring appeal of the Omaha: "To rejoice! Come! I bid you." The stress of the music of the Call is on "Zha-wa," to rejoice; the notes which carry the words "e-he," "I bid you," seem to float afar as if to reach the most distant member of the tribe with the summons. The cadence of the Call echoes itself, as the second line is like the first, only lower in tones.

When all of the camp have gathered in response to the Call, each group must stand in its appointed place and every member hold a decorated wand. Four beats of the drum are now to be given; the beats must not be loud or rapid. When the reverberations of the drum cease, absolute quiet must be maintained, each one's wand must hang downward from his right hand, while the following chant is given, sung by the leaders of the groups. The words are by John B. Tabb, the music is arranged from the Omaha invocation.

## Song No. 2

### INVOCATION

All that springeth from the sod,
Tendeth upward unto God;
All that cometh from the skies,
Urging it anon to rise.

All that spring-eth from the sod, Tend-eth up-ward un-to God;

All that com-eth from the skies, Ur-ging it a-non to rise!

This chant takes the place of the prayer sung at this point of the ceremony by the Omaha Keepers of the Tribal Sacred Pipes.   The prayer in the original has no words, vocables only are used, for the music is what carries the appeal to Wakon'da (God).

At the close of the chant two strokes of the drum should be given.   Then the leaders should sing the first line of the following song;  all the camp respond at the beginning of the second measure, and the song follows. This music is the dance song of the ceremony when all the Omaha tribe made four rhythmic advances toward the sacred tree, stopping at the close of each advance. The song was sung four times, once for each forward movement.

## Song No. 3

### APPROACH TO THE TREE

*Leaders:*          Ev'ry one lift up the branch!

*Response by all:*       Up it goes!

*Song by all:*   Dancing, singing, we like leaves sway to and fro.
Happy leaves!  Dancing leaves!
Swinging as the breezes blow,
So will we ever be
Blithe and joyous as we go.
Hi-o!

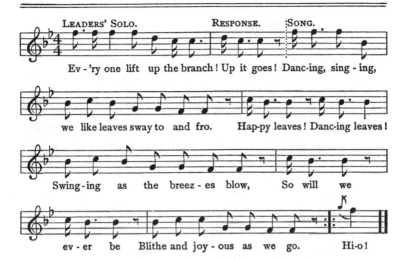

"Hi-o!" is the call given by the leaders for the dancers to pause. When this call is heard, all the branches must be at once lowered and every person stand still. After a brief pause the leaders will again sing the command, "Ev'ry one lift up the branch!" then comes the response, "Up it goes!" The song immediately follows, all the wands held high and waving in rhythm to the melody while the second advance is made. Each one of these advances should be but a few steps, on account of the limitations of space. The dancing steps, the rhythmic movements of the body and the swaying wands should give an undulating line suggestive of waving branches. The available space on the grounds should be calculated so as to permit the four approaches accompanied by the dance-song to reach a point near the tree, yet far enough to permit the forming of two circles of dancers around its base. At this point the company should divide into two parts, one part to form an inner circle and the other to form an outer circle. These two circles are now to dance around the tree, one to go from right to left, the other from left to right. At this time the leaders tie their wands to the trunk of the tree, but all the others retain their wands while they dance in these concentric circles. All should sing the dance-song, keeping time with the feet and waving the wands to the rhythm of the music. As the dance goes on, the time can be accelerated and the circles become wider and narrower, but in all these movements the rhythm of song and dance must never be broken — for the rhythm stands for the binding force of a common, social and loving life.

## Song No. 4
### DANCE AROUND THE TREE
#### I

Dance the leaves in sunlight,
Dance the leaves in dark night,
Leaves ever, ever dance on the tree,
The Tree!

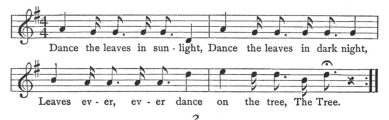

Dance the leaves in sun - light, Dance the leaves in dark night,
Leaves ev - er, ev - er dance on the tree, The Tree.

#### 2

High we lift the green branch,
Dance and wave our green branch,
Each one is a green branch of the tree,
The Tree!

3

Now we all return them,
Bind them to the tree stem,
While we sing the glad word, Unity!
O Tree!

4

Strong our hearts in daylight,
Strong our hearts in still night,
Thus the Hé-de Wa-chi bids us be,
O Tree!

This dance-song can be repeated as often as desired. When at last the leaders wish it to stop they must give the call, "Hi-o!" as they did for the pause in the Dance of Approach to the Tree.

When this signal is given, the members should toss their wands at the foot of the tree from the place where they had stopped dancing.

In the ancient Omaha ceremony the people had the vast expanse of the prairie at their disposal, yet each tribal group kept its appointed place, not only during the dance, wherein they made four approaches toward the sacred tree, but when all the groups formed into two great circles the tribal order of their relative positions was still preserved. The two circles were made up according to sex. The women and girls danced in one direction next to the pole; the men and boys formed the outer circle and danced in the opposite direction. This dance was the occasion of much hilarity and fun. Old and young danced with vigor, and great was the delight of the tribe as it spun around the emblematic tree, carrying branches. At the close of the dance all tossed the branches at the foot of the pole, leaving a mound of green on the widespreading plain.

If boys and girls take part, as they should, in this ceremony, let the girls form the inner circle and the boys the outer circle as they dance about the tree in true Omaha fashion.

In real Indian life every vocation has its accompaniment of song, no matter how homely may be the employment. So, keeping faith with that ancient American custom, let the camp be put in order after the ceremony while all sing the following song, which may be called the Clearing Up:

## Song No. 5
### THE CLEARING UP

Now is our danc-ing end-ed, Light are our hearts as our foot-steps Turn at our lead-ers' bid-ding. Safe-ly we gath-er to-geth-er Branch-es that served our play-time, Set-ting our camp all in or-der Ere to our tents we be-take us.

This scene, in which all should take part, can be made merry as well as useful.

PART II

GAMES

## INDIAN GAMES

INTRODUCTION. — All the games here presented have been played in our land for untold generations, while traces of the articles used for them have been found in the oldest remains on this continent. According to Dr. Stewart Culin, the well-known authority on Indian and other games, "There is no evidence that these games were imported into America at any time either before or after the conquest. On the other hand they appear to be the direct and natural outgrowth of aboriginal institutions in America." Dr. Culin calls attention to the reference to games in the myths of the various tribes. Among those of the Pueblo people mention is made of the divine Twins who live in the east and the west, rule the day and the night, the Summer and the Winter, "Always contending they are the original patrons of play and their games are the games now played by men." (Bureau of American Ethnology, Vol. 24, p. 32.) It would lead too far afield to follow the interesting relation between ceremonials and games, a relation that is not peculiar to the culture found on the American Continent but which obtains the world around. The environment of man in general outline is much the same everywhere; the sun ever rises in the east and sets in the west; day and night always follow each other; the winds play gently or rend with force; the rains descend in showers or fall in floods; flowers and trees spring up, come to maturity and then die. Therefore, when man has questioned Nature as to the why and the wherefore of life, similar answers have come from all parts of the earth; so it happens that man's games, which often sportively reflect his serious thoughts, show a strange similarity.

Indian games that depend upon chance, according to Dr. Culin, may be divided "into those in which the hazard depends upon the random fall of certain implements employed, like dice, and those in which it depends upon the guess or choice of the player; one is objective, the other subjective." Games of the first or objective class are generally played in silence, while those of the second or subjective class, called guessing games, are accompanied by singing. (*Ibid.*, p. 44.)

In a game where the two sides contest, as in a ball game, the sides were frequently played by two different tribes or by two villages in the same tribe. In such cases the players often went through a course of training in order to prepare them for the contest. Bathing, exercise and diet had to be followed according to prescribed custom. Among the Cherokee the partaking of rabbit was forbidden, because the animal is "timid, easily alarmed and liable to lose its wits"; so if the player ate of this dish, he might become infected with like characteristics. Mystic rites were sometimes performed to prepare the player so that he would be successful. (*Ibid.*, p. 575.)

According to the Indian belief, the pleasure of games was not restricted to mankind but was enjoyed by birds and animals. The following story from the Cherokee is told by Mr. James Mooney and quoted by Dr. Culin (*Ibid.*, pp. 578, 579):

"The animals once challenged the birds to a great ball play. The wager was accepted, the preliminaries

were arranged, and at last the contestants assembled at
the appointed spot — the animals on the ground, while
the birds took position in the tree-tops to await the
throwing up of the ball.  On the side of the animals
were the bear, whose ponderous weight bore down all
opposition; the deer, who excelled all others in running;
and the terrapin, who was invulnerable to the stoutest
blows.  On the side of the birds were the eagle, the
hawk and the great Tlániwă — all noted for their
swiftness and power of flight.  While the latter were
preening their feathers and watching every motion of
their adversaries below, they noticed two small creatures, hardly larger than mice, climbing up the tree on
which was perched the leader of the birds.  Finally
they reached the top and humbly asked the captain
to be allowed to join in the game.  The captain looked
at them a moment, and, seeing that they were four-
footed, asked them why they did not go to the animals where they properly belonged.  The little things
explained that they had done so, but had been laughed
at and rejected on account of their diminutive size.
On hearing their story the bird captain was disposed to
take pity on them, but there was one serious difficulty
in the way — how could they join the birds when they
had no wings?  The eagle, the hawk and the rest now
crowded around, and after some discussion it was decided to try and make wings for the little fellows.  But
how to do it!  All at once, by a happy inspiration, one
bethought himself of the drum which was to be used in
the dance.  The head was made of ground-hog leather,
and perhaps a corner could be cut off and utilized for

wings.  No sooner suggested than done.  Two pieces of leather taken from the drumhead were cut into shape and attached to the legs of one of the small animals, and thus originated the bat.  The ball was now tossed up and the bat was told to catch it, and his expertness in dodging and circling about, keeping the ball constantly in motion and never allowing it to fall to the ground, soon convinced the birds that they had gained a most valuable ally.  They next turned their attention to the other little creature; and now behold a worse difficulty! All their leather had been used in making wings for the bat and there was no time to send for more.  In this dilemma it was suggested that perhaps wings might be made by stretching out the skin of the animal itself. So two large birds seized him from opposite sides with their strong bills, and by tugging and pulling at his fur for several minutes succeeded in stretching the skin between the fore and hind feet until at last the thing was done, and there was the flying squirrel.  Then the bird captain, to try him, threw up the ball, when the flying squirrel, with a graceful bound, sprang off the limb and, catching it in his teeth, carried it through the air to another tree-top a hundred feet away.

" When all was ready the game began, but at the very outset the flying squirrel caught the ball and carried it up a tree, then threw it to the birds, who kept it in the air for some time, when it dropped; but just before it reached the ground the bat seized it, and by his dodging and doubling kept it out of the way of even the swiftest of the animals until he finally threw it in at the goal, and thus won the victory for the birds."

## Hazard Games

INTRODUCTORY NOTE. — The objects which are thrown or tossed in games of hazard Dr. Culin for convenience has designated as "dice" and he calls the games "dice games." (*Ibid.*, pp. 44, 45.) He found these games among one hundred and thirty tribes belonging to thirty different linguistic stocks. Throughout this wide distribution the "dice" are not only of different forms but are made from a variety of materials: split-cane; wooden or bone staves or blocks; pottery; beaver or muskrat teeth; walnut shells; persimmon, peach or plum stones. All the "dice" of whatever kind have the two sides different in color, in marking, or in both. Those of the smaller type are tossed in a basket or bowl. Those that are like long sticks, similar to arrow shafts, from which they are primarily derived, were thrown by hand. Myths of the Pueblo tribes speak of the game, in which "dice" shaped like a shaft were used, as being played by the War Gods. The split-cane "dice" were "sacrificed" on the altar sacred to the Gods of War. In this connection it is interesting to find evidence that the "dice game" of hazard was associated with the thought of war among tribes very different, both in language and customs, from the Pueblo Indians. Among the tribes living on the prairies the word used to indicate a "point" made in a "dice game" is derived from the same root as the word used to indicate an honor won on the field of battle.

Two examples of the class of games called "dice games" are here given: the first a Pueblo game played almost exclusively by men; the second a game found among the Omaha and kindred tribes and almost exclusively played by women.

## I

### PA-TOL STICK GAME

*Properties.* — Three wooden billets; a flat stone about six inches in diameter or square; forty stones about as "big as a fist" or like pieces of wood; as many sticks for markers as there are players; counters to score the game.

*Directions.* — The three billets, called pa-tol sticks, are made four and a half inches long, one inch wide and half an inch in thickness; it is important that the wood from which they are made be firm and hard. Two of the billets are plain on one side, on the other side a diagonal line is incised from the left-hand upper corner to a point about two inches below the right-hand upper corner; another diagonal line is incised from the right-hand lower corner to about two inches above the left-hand lower corner. The third pa-tol stick has the same design on one side, and on the other side the design is repeated and an additional diagonal line incised from the right-hand upper corner to the left-hand lower corner. It would be well to blacken all these incised lines in order that the designs can be readily seen during the playing of the game.

A circle, called the Pa-tol House, about three or four feet in diameter, is made by setting forty stones "about the size of a fist" so as to form the circumference. Be-

# PA-TOL STICK "DICE"

### Counts for pa-tol sticks

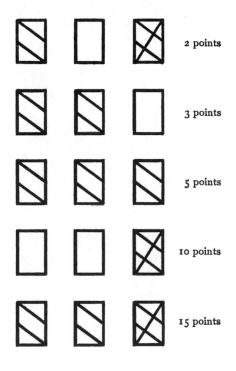

tween every tenth and eleventh stone there must be an opening of four or five inches. These openings must face the north, east, south and west; they are spoken of as "rivers." The flat stone is placed in the middle of the circle.

Each player has a marker, a small stick or twig, which is called his "horse." As many can take part in the game as conveniently can seat themselves around the pa-tol house.

The following description of the game is given by Dr. Charles F. Lummis and quoted by Dr. Culin (*Ibid.*, pp. 191, 192): "When the players have seated themselves, the first takes the pa-tol sticks tightly in his right hand, lifts them about as high as his chin and, bringing them down with a smart vertical thrust as if to harpoon the center stone, lets go of them when they are within some six inches of it. The three sticks strike the stone as one, hitting on their ends squarely, and, rebounding several inches, fall back into the circle. The manner in which they fall decides the denomination of the throw, and the different values are shown in the diagram. Although at first flush this might seem to make it a game of chance, nothing could be farther from the truth. . . . An expert pa-tol player will throw the number he desires with almost unfailing certainty by his arrangement of the sticks in his hand and the manner and force with which he strikes them down. It is a dexterity which any one may acquire by sufficient practice, and only thus. The five throw is deemed very much the hardest of all, and I have certainly found it so. [See diagram.]

"According to the number of his throw the player moves his marker an equal number of stones ahead on the circle, using one of the rivers as a starting point. If the throw is five, for instance, he lays his horse between the fourth and fifth stones and hands the pa-tol sticks to the next man.    If his throw be ten, however, as the first man's throw is very certain to be, it lands his horse in the second river, and he has another throw. The second man may make his starting point the same or another river, and may elect to run his horse around the circle in the same direction that the first is going or in the opposite.    If in the same direction, he will do his best to make a throw which will bring his horse into the same notch as that of the first man, in which case the first man is killed and has to take his horse back to the starting point, to try over again when he gets another turn.    In case the second man starts in the opposite direction — which he will not do unless an expert player — he has to calculate with a good deal of skill for the meeting, to kill and to avoid being killed by the first player.    When he starts in the same direction he is behind and runs no chance of being killed, while he has just as good a chance to kill.    But if, even then, a high throw carries him ahead of the first man — for jumping does not count either way, the only killing being when two horses come in the same notch — his rear is in danger, and he will try to run on out of the way of his pursuer as fast as possible.    The more players the more complicated the game, for each horse is threatened alike by foes that chase from behind and charge from before, and the most skilful player is liable to be sent back to the starting point several times before the game is finished, which is as soon as one horse has made the complete circuit. Sometimes the players, when very young or unskilled, agree there shall be no killing; but unless there is an explicit arrangement to that effect, killing is understood, and it adds greatly to the interest of the game."

## II

### Plum Stone Game

This game belongs to the second and non-ceremonial class of the games of hazard and is generally played by women. The Omaha type is here given, but it is similar to the game as played by kindred tribes.

*Properties.* — Five plum stones; a basket or wooden bowl; one hundred counters. The Omaha used stalks of the blue joint grass as counters, but small twigs or sticks will serve.

The plum stones should be carefully cleaned and dried. Two of the stones are burned black on both sides with a hot iron; on one side of each of these stones a crescent is marked, and between the lines of the figure the black is carefully scraped so as to leave a clear design of a new moon on a background of black. On the other side of these two stones a star, four or five pointed, is drawn and all the black within the lines is scraped off, leaving a brown star on a background of black. The other three stones are each burned black all over on one side; the other side is left the natural color of the stones. These stones can be prepared in camp, but the basket or wooden bowl will probably have to be furnished from outside.

*Directions.* — Two players to one basket or bowl. The game is generally one hundred points.

The two players sit opposite and have the basket or bowl between them, with the five plum stones lying in the bottom. The one hundred counters are within reach at one side. As points are made, the winner takes a corresponding number of counters from the general pile and lays them beside her on the side opposite to the general pile; when this is exhausted, then the winner takes her counters from the winnings of her opponent. Whoever wins all of the one hundred points has the game.

Lots should be drawn to decide who shall have the first play. The one who wins the first play takes the bowl or basket by the rim with both hands and gives it a toss sufficient to throw.up all the stones, but not violent enough to make them fall outside the bowl or basket; such a throw would not count. If the throw is not such as to move all the stones, make them turn and all move about within the bowl, that throw will not count.

The following are the combinations that count, that is, make points:

Two moons and three whites (natural color) = 10 points.

Two stars and three blacks = 10 points.

One moon, one star and three whites (natural color) = 1 point.

One moon, one star and three blacks = 1 point.

No other combinations count anything in the game. As will be seen, there are a number which cannot be counted. If one tosses the bowl and the stones fall in such manner as to make a combination that does not count, there is no forfeit; the player merely fails to score any points.   The player who wins a point, or points, keeps on tossing the bowl until she fails to make a point. She must then let her opponent toss the bowl, who will keep tossing the bowl as long as she can win a point. There are players among the Indian women who are very skilful and are able to make the stones fall frequently in the combinations that win ten points.

## Guessing Games

INTRODUCTORY NOTE. — Games of the "subjective" class, designated as guessing games by Dr. Culin, were generally accompanied by singing.   There is a great variety in the games of this class, and five examples drawn from different sections of the country are here presented.

Indian games of this character do not always depend so much on chance as on the quickness of vision and skilful manipulation by the players.   In games of this class the Indians never make random motions, all their movements, whether of the body, the feet, the hands or arms, being always in strict accord with the accompanying song, while the drama implied in the game is acted out, at the same time, more or less clearly.   In these games the Indian players seem to be impelled by a common rhythmic and dramatic impulse, making a unity that enhances the interest and pleasure excited by the game.

# I

## PU–IN

INTRODUCTORY NOTE. — This was a favorite game among the natives of the Northeastern States; its "strange whimsies" were first mentioned by William Wood in his book, "New England Prospect," published in London, 1634. It is probable that some form of this game still persists among the scattered descendants of those nearly extinct tribes, but it is not likely that at the present day the victor would proclaim his prowess, as was formerly done, by wearing in the holes of his ears the counters that marked the number of his successful guesses.

*Properties.* — A number of wheat or other straws cut about a foot long; a mat or blanket; a pointed staff for the Leader.

*Directions.* — Ten straws must be laid aside as counters for each player. The rest of the straws are separated into tens and each ten tied with a wisp, making a bundle; one bundle must have eleven straws. There should be as many bundles as players. The bundles must all be tied alike. The game consists in guessing which bundle has the eleven straws. The number of guesses allowed in a game must be fixed upon before starting to play.

All the bundles are thrown in a heap upon the center of the mat. The Leader, who is generally chosen by lot, leads the players to the mat containing the bundles. Each player holds in his left hand his ten counters and follows the Leader with his staff as he moves around the mat from left to right, while all sing the following song, taking steps to the rhythm of the music:

### GAME SONG

Ah   hey  they hey,  Ah hey  they hey,  Ah  hey  they hey,  Ah

hey  hey  ah  hey,  Ah  they hey  they  they,  Ah

When the Leader strikes his staff on the ground every player must stop just where he happens to be, stoop and pick up a bundle with his right hand and begin to wave it above his head and sway his body to the time of the song. When the Leader points with his staff to a player, that person must make a guess. As he scans the waving bundles he points with his left hand that holds his counters to the bundle which he thinks contains the eleven straws. If the guess proves to be correct, the guesser puts one of his counters in his hair or behind his ear. At once all bundles must be thrown in a heap on the mat. The Leader then moves forward by the left, followed by the players, every one singing and keeping time with the song. When the Leader strikes the ground with his staff, all halt. Each player immediately seizes a bundle, holds it aloft and begins to wave it. The Leader designates with his staff a person who must guess. If the guess is wrong, the guesser drops one of his counters on the mat and the Leader points to another player who must guess. If he loses, he drops one of his counters on the mat; the guessing goes on as described, until some one is successful and puts a counter in his hair, when the bundles are all thrown on the mat and the play begins again as before. Should the person designated by the Leader to guess think that he holds the bundle with eleven straws, he must point it at the Leader. If this surmise is correct, the person guessing puts a counter in his hair and all bundles are again thrown on the mat.

In this way the game proceeds until some player has won the requisite number of counters and has them all standing in his hair. Throughout the game the singing must be kept up, accompanied by rhythmic movements of the feet and the body, the players acting as though searching among the tall grass for a desired clump. When a point is won, the Leader should shout out the counter won, without interrupting the song or the play. Among the Indians the game, once started, is kept going without halt or break in the song or the movements. The calling out of the winnings in no way disturbs the singing or the playing.

The victor should wear his successful counters in his hair the rest of the day, if possible.

## II

### ATÁ–A–KUT

INTRODUCTORY NOTE. — This game is played among one of the basket making tribes of California. As not infrequently occurs in Indian games, there is in this pastime a reflection both of the environment and of the vocations of the people who used it. The drama or theme of the play is the search for a particular reed, which for the purpose of the game is marked in a special way.

*Properties.* — A mat or blanket and about fifty reeds; the reeds should be similar in thickness and about a foot long.

*Directions.* — The number of points which shall constitute winning the game should first be agreed upon; if ten be the number, then twenty reeds should be set aside as counters and the rest used as game-reeds. All of these latter must be alike save one, and that reed must have a black band about an inch or so wide painted around the middle, that is, midway between the two ends of the reed. It is this particular reed that must be detected or its location guessed.

The mat or blanket should be laid east and west. The two players sit opposite each other, one near the northern edge of the mat, the other near the southern edge. The counters are divided in half, one-half put at the eastern end of the mat, the other half at the western. The counters at the east belong to the player sitting at the north, those at the west to the player at the south. Two singers stand back of each player. The spectators are grouped about the mat, but must not be too near the players. Lots are drawn to decide which player shall "hold the reeds." The player who loses the chance to "hold the reeds" becomes the one who is to be the guesser.

All the game-reeds, including the reed with the black

band painted on it, are thrown in a pile in the center of the mat or blanket. The player who is to "hold the reeds" gathers all the game-reeds in his hands, brings them behind his back, where he shuffles and divides the reeds into two bunches, one for each hand. When he is ready to bring his hands forward, each one with a bunch of reeds grasped by the middle, the two singers standing behind him start the following song:

GAME SONG

He ah  e  ya  ha  e  tha,  He ah  e  ya  ha  e  tha,  He ah  e  ya  ha  e  tha,  He ah  e  ya  ha  e  tha,  He ah  e  ya  ha  e  tha.

When the music begins, the player holding the reeds sways his body from side to side, moves his arms and hands with the reeds and simulates being blown by the winds. The opposite player, by the movements of body and arms, indicates that he is pushing his way through tall reeds tossed by the wind, searching for something he desires to find. Both players in all their movements must keep in rhythm of the song, observe strict time and strive to make their actions tell the story plainly. The guesser through all his motions must keep his eyes on the bunches held by his opponent, seeking for an indication to show which one contains the marked reed. When he is ready to guess he extends both arms toward the bunch he has fixed upon, as if to grasp it. At this action the holder of the reeds must open his hand and let the reeds of that bundle fall on the mat. The guesser then searches among the spilled reeds for the one that is marked; if he finds it, he holds it up so that all can see that his guess has been correct and the reed discovered. The two singers who stand behind him give the victory shout, go to his pile of counters, take one and place it at his right hand, then the reeds of the other bunch are thrown by the holder on the mat, so that all the game-reeds are lying in the center, as at the beginning of the game.

The player who made the successful guess now picks up the game-reeds and behind his back shuffles and divides them. When he is ready to bring forward his two hands holding the reeds, the two singers standing behind him begin the Game Song, while he waves the bunches, acting what is now his rôle, that of the reeds being blown about by the winds. The other player now becomes the guesser and must act as though he were searching among the blown reeds for the one he desires.

The player who "holds the reeds" is thought to have the advantage; that is why lots are drawn at the beginning to decide who shall have that part in the game. The player holding the reeds aims to make the guessing as difficult as possible by deftness in hiding the banded reed, so as to keep his advantage.

Every time a guess is made the reeds of the bunch

guessed must at once be dropped on the mat, that all may see the reeds while the guesser searches among them for the marked reed. If he cannot find it, the singers who stand behind him call out that a point has been lost, take a counter from his pile and place it at the right hand of the player holding the reeds, who at once drops all the game-reeds on the middle of the mat, to be again taken up by him, shuffled and divided behind his back, when he resumes the waving of the bunches of reeds blown by the wind and the guesser who lost starts to make another guess. Should he be successful, the counter he had lost would be taken back and placed at his right hand. In this manner counters lost can be reclaimed, until one or the other of the players has won and been able to hold the number of counters required for the game.

The presentation of the little drama of this game rhythmically affords an opportunity for considerable dramatic action and yields pleasure both to the performers and to the spectators. This game was much played among the tribes where it was known.

## III

### Hand Game

Introductory Note. — This game, Dr. Culin states, is played among eighty-one Indian tribes of the United States. The game bears different names in the various languages of these tribes. Hand Game is a descriptive term and not a translation of any native name; it refers to the fact that the object is held in the hand during the play. The following form of this game is the way it was formerly played among the Nez Percé Indians of the State of Idaho. Lewis and Clark, who were the first white men to record their meeting with these Indians, mention this game, and Capt. Bonneville gives an account of it when he visited the tribe during the third decade of the last century.

*Properties.* — A bone or wooden bead about two inches in length and half an inch in thickness; thirty counting sticks (these are sometimes spoken of as arrows, and there are indications that they were once arrows — the arrows of the twin gods); a mat oblong in shape; two logs or pieces of board about the length of the mat, and as many sticks (to be used as drum-sticks) as players can sit on one side of the mat.

*Directions.* — The mat should be laid east and west, the logs or boards put on the north and south edges and the counting sticks placed in two piles of fifteen each on the ends of the mat. The players sit on the ground, a row on each side of the mat to the north and south. Lots are drawn to decide which side shall have the bead "in hand." The Leader and the singers must always stand behind the row of players who have the bead "in hand." The opposite side must have the drum-sticks and beat on the log or board in time with the singers.

When the players are seated in two rows, one on each side of the mat, the Leader hands the bead to a player on the side that has drawn the right to have the bead "in hand," and then takes his place beside the singers, who stand behind that row, and starts the following song. All in that row join in the singing.

HAND GAME SONG

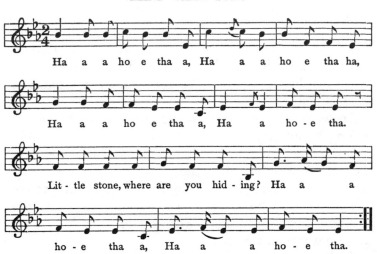

Ha   a   a   ho   e   tha   a,   Ha   a   a   ho   e   tha   ha,

Ha   a   a   ho   e   tha   a,   Ha   a   ho - e   tha.

Lit - tle   stone, where   are   you   hid - ing?   Ha   a   a

ho - e   tha   a,   Ha   a   a   ho - e   tha.

The players on the opposite side, who are to guess who is hiding the bead, at once begin to beat the time of the song on the log or board that is in front of them, on the edge of the mat, and at the same time they must watch the other side where the players are trying to pass the bead from one hand to the other and from one person to another without exposing the bead to view.  In all these actions the movements of hands, arms and body must be rhythmical and in time with the song.  All the players in the row that has the bead "in hand" must act as if each one either had the bead or was trying to pass it on, whether he actually has the bead or does not have it.

When one on the opposite side thinks he detects the whereabouts of the bead and is willing to risk a guess, he points his drum-stick to the hand he thinks has the bead and cries, "Hi-i!" and the hand indicated must be immediately opened so that all may see whether the guess is correct or not. If the bead is seen to be in the opened hand, the Leader calls out, "Success!" and goes to the pile of counting sticks belonging to the side of the guesser, takes one and stands it in the ground in front of the successful guesser. The Leader then hands the bead to the player who has won and proceeds to gather the drum-sticks and distribute them to the players on the opposite side. The singers pass around and take their places behind the row of players who now have the bead "in hand." When all are in readiness, the Leader starts the song again and the players begin their movements of secretly passing the bead, while the other side beat time with their drum-sticks on the log or board in front of them. The side that has the bead "in hand" always does the singing, led by the Leader and singers, who must stand at the rear of the row having the bead.

If a guess is incorrect the Leader goes to the pile of counting sticks that belongs to the side which has the drum-sticks, takes a counting stick and thrusts it in the ground in front of the row opposite to the guesser; that means one lost to his side. The bead in that instance remains on the same side until it is won by the opposite side through a successful guess.

In this manner the game goes on until one side or the other has won all the thirty counting sticks and become the victor in the game.

IV

## Hiding the Disks

Introductory Note. — This game, known under a variety of names, is a favorite among the Indian tribes living on the North Pacific Coast. The disks, always of an uneven number, are made of wood and ornamented with designs composed of segments of circles with groupings of dots. Some of the markings are regarded as cabalistic, and there are men who claim to have a knowledge of spells that will bring luck to the disks they ornament and treat; such disks are considered valuable and often command a high price. All of the disks in a set that is used in this game are ornamented alike except one; this must be different from the others. It may be decorated with red, for the sun, or with a dark color almost black, for the night. This disk is frequently called the "chief," and the aim of the game is to guess in which pile of disks the "chief" is hidden.

*Properties.* — A mat on which the game is played; a small mat on which the counting or tally-sticks are put; a board that is to serve as a drum; four drum-sticks; nine wooden disks about two and a half inches in diameter. The designs on the nine disks, the twenty tally-sticks and the four drum-sticks should be in color or burned into the wood. Eight of the disks should be decorated alike; the ninth must be different and have either red or brown as the predominating color; this disk is the "chief." A bundle of excelsior is to be the substitute for the fiber of cedar bark which is used by the Indians of the Northwest Coast when playing this game;

if excelsior is not available, dry leaves or some other dry material might be substituted, within which, or under which, the disks could be hidden. All the articles used in this game except the mats should be made in camp.

*Directions.* — An uneven number of players is required for this game. The mat is laid east and west; at a little distance back to the northwest the small mat is placed and on it are put the twenty tally-sticks. In a line with the small mats to the northeast is laid the board around which the four singers and drummers sit. The bundle of excelsior, or whatever material is used in its place, together with the nine disks, is put at the western end of the mat; before these is the place for the player who is to hide the disks. On the northern and southern side of the mat sit the players who are to guess where the "chief" is hidden, three or four on a side. The messenger stands at the eastern end of the mat facing the player who is to hide the disks. Lots should be drawn to determine who of the six or eight players are to sit on the northern side and who on the southern side. The player who is to do the hiding of the disks can be either selected or drawn by lot. Whoever takes this part in the game should be capable of considerable dramatic action. Among the Indians the person who does the hiding of the disks personifies one who practices magic; he makes passes over the disks and the cedar fiber under which the disks are hidden, makes signs and movements, and does what he can to throw a spell of confusion over those who are to guess where the "chief" is hidden.

When the players about the mat, the singers about the

board drum and the messenger standing at the eastern
end of the mat are all in readiness, the singers begin the
following song, keeping time by beating with their
drum-sticks on the board drum; the players about the
mat join in the singing.

HIDING THE DISKS

E ya   ha   e   ha   e   tha,    E ya   ha   e   ha   e   tha,

E ya   ha   e   ha   e   tha,    E ya   ha   e   ha   e   tha,

E ya   ha   e   ha   e   tha,    E ya   ha   e   ha   e   tha,

E ya   ha   e   ha   e   tha,    E ya   ha   e   ha   e   tha,

E ya   ha   e   ha   e   tha.

The player at the western end of the mat opens the
bundle of excelsior or other material and spreads it on
the mat and then puts all the nine disks under the material, making many movements as he does so, all of
which must be in rhythm with the song, rolling the disks
about under the material and finally dividing them into

two parts, well covered up by the material. He continues to make passes with his hands as though invoking mysterious forces and to shuffle around the two piles of material in which the disks are hidden. Suddenly a player points to one of the piles; the player at the end ceases to shuffle and sends the disks concealed in the pile rolling down the mat to the messenger standing at the other end, who looks to see if the "chief" is among the disks rolled toward him. If he finds it, all of the players on the side of the guesser give the victory shout and the messenger goes to the small mat, brings one of the tally-sticks and stands it before the successful guesser. Then the messenger rolls the disks back to the other end of the mat where the person sits who hides the disks. That player begins again his passes and movements as he mixes together the nine disks and hides them under the material; then he divides the disks and the material under which they are hidden into two piles, shuffles them about until a player points to a pile, when he at once stops shuffling and sends the disks under the pile pointed at rolling down the mat to the messenger. If the "chief" is not found among the disks, the side to which the unsuccessful guesser belongs loses a point, and the messenger takes from the small mat a tally-stick and stands it at the end of the row of players on the opposite side. The disks are then sent spinning over the mat to the player who hides them. He mixes up the disks, hides them, shuffles the piles until another guess is made. If that guess should be by a player on the side that had just lost a point, and the guess prove to be successful — that is, the pile pointed at contain the "chief" — then the messenger takes the tally-stick that had been put at the end of the row of the opposite side and stands it in front of the successful guesser.  He could not take back a tally-stick that had been won by a guess unless all the tally-sticks had been taken from the small mat.  One side or the other must win twenty points to be victor in the game.  In the process of winning the game the tally-sticks may therefore be taken back and forth before one side wins the entire twenty.

The victory shout is given only when a successful guess is made.  The singing stops at a victory shout and is resumed as soon as the disks are rolled back to the player who hides the disks.  He must be careful to keep all his dramatic actions and movements of hands, arms, body and head in rhythmic accord with the song.  The steps and movements of the messenger must also be in time with the song.

## V

### I-OU'-TIN

INTRODUCTORY NOTE.— This game belongs to the class of guessing games.  The form here presented is adapted from the game as played by the Omaha, Otoe, Ponca and Pawnee tribes, among whom it is a favorite.

*Properties.* — A standard, or the camp flagstaff can be used; a blanket or rug; three official scarfs, one blue, one green, one white; two wands, one decorated with blue and the other with green; eight tally-rods, ornamented at one end with red tassels; two small balls of

# DIAGRAM FOR I-OU'-TIN

1   Standard
2   Blanket or rug
3   Drum
4   Wands
5   Tally-rods and balls
6   Custodian
7   Judges
8   Guessers
9   Singers
10  Players

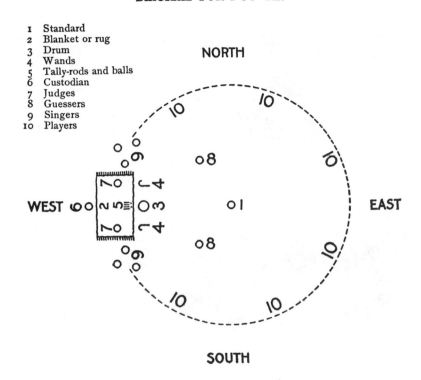

a light, soft material, hair or wool; a drum; six deco-rated drum-sticks; rosettes of blue and of green; strips of blue and green paper.

*Directions.* — A fairly level open space large enough for a circle of from twenty to thirty feet in diameter is marked upon the ground, in the center of which the standard is planted. Directly west and on a line with the standard the blanket or rug is spread. In front of the rug and on a line with the standard the drum is set. At a little distance on each side of the drum the two wands are thrust in the ground, the one decorated with blue to the north, the one with green to the south. On the rug back of the drum the eight tally-rods are laid in a bunch, with the butts of the rods toward the east. At the butts of the rods are placed the two little balls.

The players draw lots as to which side they are to be-long. This is done by putting the green and blue strips of paper in a receptacle and each one drawing a strip. Those who draw blue belong to the north side; those who draw green, to the south side. Each player must then fasten a rosette, of the color of the side to which he or she belongs, on the shoulder; those who belong to the north side must put the blue rosette on the right shoulder, and those who belong to the south side must put the green rosette on the left shoulder.

*Officers.* — Two Judges; a Custodian; two Guessers; six Singers.

The players on the north side choose from among their number one who is to be their Judge; the players on the south side choose one for their Judge. It is the duty of the Judges to select the Custodian, the six Singers, the two Guessers; to preserve order, decide when there are disputes, and to lead in the opening ceremony.

The Custodian has charge of all the properties, must place them as directed, move the drum from side to side, and at the close of the game gather all the articles required for the game and put them in a place of safe keeping for use at another time. The Custodian wears the official white scarf tied about the waist. This officer does not wear any rosette, as the Custodian does not belong to either side but to all who take part in the game.

The Judge on the north side must wear the blue official scarf. This is crossed over the breast from the right shoulder, on which is the blue rosette, to the waist on the left side, where it is tied. The Judge on the south side wears the green official scarf. This is crossed over the breast from the left shoulder, where is the green rosette, to the waist at the right side, where it is tied.

The six Singers, three for each side, sit in an open group on the ground near the ends of the rug, those wearing blue rosettes on the north and those wearing green rosettes on the south side. The players take their seats on the ground on the line of the circle, those wearing blue rosettes on the north half, those wearing green rosettes on the south half of the circle.

When all are in their places the Custodian leads the two Judges to the rug, on which they are to sit a little back of the wands — blue to the North, green to the South. The Custodian then takes up the tally-rods, gives four to each of the Judges and retires to stand back of the rug, behind the Judges, ready for duty.

Up to this moment laughing and talking goes on among the players, but as the Custodian divides the tally-rods and hands them to the Judges instant silence falls on all present.

### The Opening Ceremony

The two Judges rise in their places. The north side Judge holds the four tally-rods in his right hand, the south side Judge holds the four tally-rods in his left hand; the two then walk abreast to the standard. There they face the North, move forward a few steps, pause, and each Judge holds up his tally-rods to the North, while all the players on both sides of the circle sing the following song:

### Song

I

Hail! O North! Thy wind send
To blow care away,
To bring joy to-day;
Makes Eyes keen,
Make Hands swift for play.

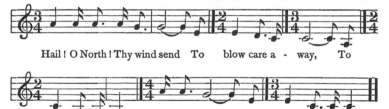

Hail! O North! Thy wind send To blow care a - way, To
bring joy to-day; Make eyes keen, Make hands swift for play.

At the close of the stanza the two Judges lower their tally-rods, turn, walk toward the East, pause, then elevate their tally-rods, and all the players sing the second stanza.

*2*

Hail! O East! Thy wind send
To blow care away,
To bring joy to-day;
Makes Eyes keen,
Make Hands swift for play.

At the close of the stanza the two Judges lower their tally-rods, turn, walk toward the South, pause, again elevate their tally-rods, while all the players sing the third stanza.

*3*

Hail! O South! Thy wind send
To blow care away,
To bring joy to-day;
Make Eyes keen,
Make Hands swift for play.

At the close of this stanza the two Judges lower their tally-rods, turn, walk toward the West, pause, once more elevate their tally-rods, and all the players join in singing the fourth stanza.

*4*

Hail! O West! Thy wind send
To blow care away,
To bring joy to-day;
Make Eyes keen,
Make Hands swift for play.

At the close of the song the Judges lower their tally-rods and walk to the rug, where they take their appointed seats behind the respective wands. They then lay all the tally-rods on the space between them.

## The Contest

A contest now takes place between the two persons chosen by the Judges to be the two Guessers, one for each side, to decide which shall begin the game. The Judge for the north side calls the name of the person chosen to be the Guesser for that side and the Custodian escorts him to his place within the circle. The Judge for the south side calls the name of the person chosen to be Guesser for that side, and the Custodian escorts him to his place within the circle. The Custodian then gives to each the wand belonging to his side and also one of the small balls.

The Guesser from the north side hides his ball in one of his hands, shifting it behind his back, then he holds out both hands in front of him with all the fingers closed except the index finger, which is extended as if pointing to the other Guesser. Both hands and forearms must be rhythmically moved up and down. The south side Guesser watches for a moment and then points with his wand to the hand he thinks has the ball. As soon as he points to a hand, it must be immediately opened, palm upward. Should the ball be in the other hand, it must be shown to be lying there. If the guess was correct, the ball being in the hand pointed at, it counts one. Three correct guesses must be made by one of the Guessers in order to secure for his side the right to open the game. In this contest the Guessers must alternate, first the north side Guesser, then the south side Guesser, and so on until one of the Guessers has won three correct guesses. That decides it. His side is to hide the ball and the other side's Guesser is to do the guessing.

## THE GAME

The Custodian takes the drum from its position in front of the rug, carries it to the side of the successful Guesser and sets it before the three Singers who are to lead in the singing of the song belonging to that side of the circle of players. Every one on that side must sing the song as they hide the balls. Only those on the side that is hiding the balls sing. They can only sing the song that belongs to their side.

### SONG FOR THE NORTH SIDE

### SONG FOR THE SOUTH SIDE

There are no words for either of these songs. The vocables given are those used with these songs when the Indians sing them as they hide the balls.

The Custodian takes the two balls from the Guessers and hands them to two persons designated by the Guesser who has won the right for that side to begin. The two persons designated must be two who are sitting together. They each take a ball, and they must hide the balls in the same manner as did the Guessers during the contest. The fingers of the hands are closed, all but the index finger, which is extended as if pointing. The hands and arms move up and down and also from one side to the other; all of these movements must be in exact time to the song and the drum-beats. These swaying, rhythmic movements are pleasing to the eye and add to the enjoyment of the game. While the two persons having the balls are hiding them, swaying their hands and arms, the Guesser, who is of the opposite side, is watching intently the hands of the players. When he is ready to make a guess he points his wand to where he thinks the balls are — directly in front, if he suspects the balls to be in the two inside hands. If he thinks the balls are in the two outside hands, he points his wand to one of the hands and extends his empty hand toward the other; in that case the Guesser stands with both of his arms extended. As soon as the Guesser points with his wand, the hands indicated must be at once opened, palms upward, so that all can see whether the guess is right or wrong.

Every correct guess counts one for the side of the Guesser. As soon as a correct guess is made, the Judge for that side takes up one of the tally-rods and lays it toward his side; this shows that a point has been won for that side.   If the guess is wrong, the Judge for the other side takes up one of the tally-rods and lays it over on his side.   The other side has lost one, while his side has gained by the other's loss.

To win a sweep, all the eight tally-rods must be gained by one side.   Three sweeps by a side gives that side the game.

Whenever a sweep is made the balls are handed over to the Custodian.   The two Judges rise, go to the standard, stand there, one facing North (his side), the other the South (his side).   The two Guessers go to the standard, stand there, one facing East, the other West. All the winning side rise, go toward the standard and form a circle around it.   There they sing the Victory Song.

## VICTORY SONG

Drum-beats

Hi ya ho hi ya ho hi ya ho ah

ho   Hi ya ho hi ya ho hi ya ho ah

ho   Hi ya ho hi ya ho hi ya ho ah ho.

As they sing they sway their arms as though hiding the balls, and dance to the rhythm of the song. Four times they dance around the standard and sing the Victory Song. All movements must be in time with the song. At the close of the fourth circuit of the standard, all return to their appointed places and the game is resumed.

The Custodian takes up the drum, carries it to the side that has just danced and sets it before the three Singers of that side. The Guesser, who is of the opposite side, designates the two who are to hide the balls and the game proceeds as described above.

Whenever a side that has been hiding the balls fails three times to elude the Guesser, then the Custodian takes the drum from that side and carries it to the other side of the circle, puts it before the Singers and gives the balls as directed. Sometimes there are disputes as to these transfers and as to the points lost; three must be lost to secure a transfer. It then becomes the duty of the Judges to decide.

With every transfer of the drum the song changes. The balls and the right to sing go together, but the song belonging to one side must not be sung by the other side. The songs are not interchangeable.

This game is provocative of fun and merriment as well as dexterity of hand and quickness of vision. It also presents a very pretty spectacle. It is greatly enjoyed by Indian men, women and children. It has also found favor with merrymakers of our own race.

# Ball Games

## INTRODUCTION

Indian ball games have one feature not found in the ball games as played by us; that is, with the Indian the ball is never pitched and tossed by hand during the play. At the opening of an Indian game the ball must be tossed by hand, but after that the ball is struck by a racket, stick or club and in that way sent from player to player and on to the goal. An exception to this general rule is found in an Omaha ball game given in the following pages.

The opening ceremony requires the ball to be handled and moved in a peculiar and ceremonial manner by the hand of the Umpire before he tosses it up for the beginning of the actual play.

The balls used by the Indians are of different materials — buckskin stuffed with hair; formed from roots, such as the wild-grape vine; wood; bladder netted with sinew; and in a few instances, of bone or stone.

Three ball games are here given.

## I

## BALL AND RACKET

INTRODUCTORY NOTE. — The game in which the ball is struck with a racket is almost exclusively played by men, but there are tribes where it is played by women, and one tribe, cited by Dr. Culin, where it is played by men and women together. The form of ball game where the racket is used was less widely distributed over the country than some others.  It was most frequently found among tribes living near the Atlantic Coast and in the region of the Great Lakes.  It had a limited range on the Pacific.  There are two forms of the Racket Ball Game, one where a single racket is used and the other where two rackets are employed to catch the ball.  The latter form is peculiar to the tribes formerly living in the Southern States.  The game here given ispresented as it is played among the Chippewa tribes dwelling in Minnesota.

*Properties*. — A ball, not too hard and the size usually employed for cricket.  As many rackets as there are players.  Red and yellow head-bands equally divided as to number and enough for all the players.

*Directions*. — The field should be as large as the camp ground will permit.  At the extreme East of the field a tall pole should be set as a goal and a like pole at the West for the other goal.  To the pole at the East a red streamer should be tied and a yellow streamer to the pole at the West.  These poles should be practically in line and as distant from each other as it is conveniently possible to set them.  The rackets should be made in camp.  A racket can be made from a sapling cut at such length that when the racket is completed it will be 26 inches long.  One end of the sapling is whittled flat on one side for a sufficient length to be bent round to the shaft or handle so as to form the rim of the circular receptacle which is to receive the ball.  Sometimes both sides of this bent portion of the sapling are made flat.  The end of this flat end where it curls round upon the shaft or handle must be bound firmly to the shaft with thongs or heavy twine. Holes are sometimes bored through the rim and the thongs or twine are passed through them and woven into a loose netting to form a bottom to the coiled end, making a shallow cup-shaped receptacle in which to catch or hold the ball. The rackets are not difficult to make. Each lad should make his own racket and mark the stem with some device by which he can identify it should he drop it during the play. Care should be taken when making the racket to have the cup-shaped receptacle at the end of the shaft of such size as to hold the ball without its rolling about, in which case it would be easily dropped when being carried on a run; yet it must be large enough to catch and hold the ball as it is flying about. The players should be divided into two parties by casting lots. Those who belong to the east goal should wear red head-bands; those who have the west goal should wear yellow head-bands. An Umpire must be selected. The ball must strike one of the goal posts to make a point; the number of points that shall constitute the game should be agreed upon. Two players, one from each side, stand near each goal. One helps the ball for his side; the other hinders the ball when near the goal by tossing it back into the field again so that his side may catch it.

## THE GAME

The four players stand at their posts beside the two goals; all the others gather in the field. The Umpire takes the ball and goes to a place as near the center of the field as possible. All being in readiness, he throws the ball with force straight up in the air.   Every player watches the ball and makes ready to try and catch it in his racket when it descends.   If one succeeds in catching the ball, he runs at full speed toward his goal, holding his racket so that the ball will not fall out.   The other players rush after him, trying to strike his racket and dislodge the ball.   If he is hard pressed he may try to toss the ball to a player on his side who has a clearer space; if the ball is caught by the player to whom it was sent, then all the players turn upon the new holder of the ball and try to block his progress.   In this game care must be taken never to strike the arm or body of a player; only the racket should be struck.   There is danger of receiving injuries if this rule is not strictly observed.

Perhaps one of the most difficult feats in this game is when a player has brought his ball near to the goal to so turn his racket while it holds the ball as to send the ball with such force that it will strike the post squarely and not miss the goal.   The difficulty is owing to the horizontal position of the racket when holding the ball. Of course, the keenest playing is about the goal, where the guard of the side opposite to the player does his best to catch the ball on its way to the post and send it back into the field.

The ball should not be allowed to touch the ground from the time the Umpire throws it into the air until it falls at the pole after a point has been made by the ball striking the post.   It is the duty of the Umpire to go to the pole, mark the score, return with the ball to the center of the field, where he again sends it up into the air, and the game starts afresh for a second point to be made.

This game is good sport; it develops and requires skill, agility and strength.

## II

### TA–BÉ

INTRODUCTORY NOTE. — This ball game was known to a number of tribes that formerly lived on the prairies, and called by different names. The game as here given is as it was played among the Omaha. The opening of the game was ceremonial. The person who performed the opening ceremony had to belong to the tribal group that had charge of the rites pertaining to the Wind, for the figure outlined on the ground by the movements of the ball in the opening ceremony was one of the symbols of the Wind. The Wind when spoken of ceremonially was called the Four Winds, one for each of the four points of the compass. These Four Winds were regarded as the messengers of the Giver of Life, known as Wakon'da by the Omaha and kindred tribes. The recognition of man's connection with the forces of Nature did not disturb the pleasure of the Indian when entering upon a game; on the contrary, it tended to enhance his happiness by bringing to his mind his dependence upon Wakon'da, together with the feeling of being in accord with the power represented by the Wind.

*Properties.* — A ball about three or four inches in diameter; the Omaha and kindred tribes made the ball out of the root of the wild-grape vine. As many sticks as

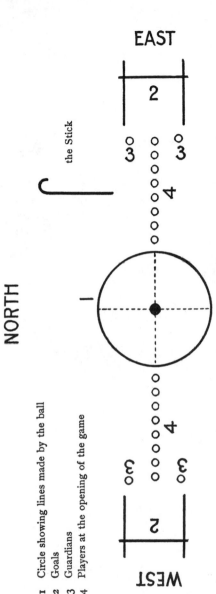

the Stick

EAST

NORTH

SOUTH

WEST

1 Circle showing lines made by the ball
2 Goals
3 Guardians
4 Players at the opening of the game

**DIAGRAM OF THE TA-BÉ**

there are players, the sticks to be about three feet long and crooked over at one end. Each stick should be marked by some design invented by its owner, so that each player can identify his stick.

*Directions.* — A wide open field is best for this game. Two goals, one at the East, the other at the West. The goals are each made by two posts with a cross piece on top. The path of the ball is East and West.

The officers of the game are: an Umpire, four Guardians of the Path. Two of the Guardians of the Path stand at the eastern goal and two at the western goal. The two Guardians at a goal represent the two sides; one wears a yellow streamer or badge, the color of the West; the other wears a red streamer or badge, the color of the East. A red streamer is tied to the goal at the East and a yellow streamer to the goal at the West. It is the duty of the one who wears the color of the goal by which he stands to try and help the ball through the goal when it comes in that direction, and it is the duty of the one who wears the color of the opposite goal to prevent the ball from going through and to send it back into the field or toward the other goal.

The players on the two sides are chosen in the following manner: The person who is to act as Umpire and to perform the opening ceremony must sit in a circle drawn on the ground, about six feet in diameter, and face either the North or the South. All the sticks are placed before him in a bunch. He is then blindfolded. After that he picks up a stick with each hand and lays down the stick that he has in his right hand on his left side, the stick that he has in his left hand he lays down on his right side. When he has finished dividing the sticks in this manner they are in two bunches, one toward the East and the other toward the West. The blindfold is then removed. When that is done, all the players run to the two heaps and each takes his own stick, recognizing it by the design marked or cut upon the stick. All those whose sticks were in the pile to the East must tie on a badge or streamer the color of the East, red. All those whose sticks were in the bunch toward the West must tie on the color of the West, yellow.

All the players must now stand in two lines. One line starts from the circle and extends directly toward the goal at the East; all in this line must be only those whose sticks were in the east pile and who have on the color of the East, red. The other line starts from the circle and stretches out toward the west goal, and is composed of those whose sticks were in the west pile and who have on the color of the West, yellow. The four Guardians of the Path take their places. The Umpire wears no color. All being in readiness, the Umpire advances to the middle of the circle.

## THE OPENING CEREMONY

The Umpire places the ball in the exact center of the circle, then he gently urges it with his stick in a line toward the North until it reaches the edge of the circle. There he picks it up and puts it back in the center of the circle. Again he gently pushes it with his stick along a line toward the South until the edge of the circle is reached, when he returns the ball to the center of the circle with his hand. In the same manner as before he sends the ball slowly along a line to the West. When the edge of the circle is reached he picks up the ball and returns it to the center. Once more the ball is moved in a line, this time to the East; when it touches the line of the circle it is picked up as before and placed in the center of the circle. The symbolic figure that has thus been made is that of a circle within which two straight lines cross each other at right angles; the circle is divided into four quarters, one for each of the Four Winds.

## THE GAME

Every player now stands at attention, with his stick ready for action. The Umpire pauses a moment at the center of the circle, then he picks up the ball lying there and throws it into the air as high as he can. All the players, who have watched the throw, run in the direction where the ball seems likely to descend, in order to have a chance to strike it toward one of the goals.

To win the game the ball must be sent through a goal; to strike it so that it goes over or around the goal does not count. The ball must be made to take a straight line, to "make a straight path" through a goal, then the game is won. When a good shot is made, all on the side of the one who made the stroke should send up a shout. When the goal is won the winning side should give the victory cry of the game, "Ta-bé!"

## III

### DOUBLE–BALL GAME

INTRODUCTORY NOTE. — Some stories credit the Moon as the giver of this game to the women, by whom it is exclusively played throughout the United States except among the tribes in Northern California, where the men use the game. There are indications that the Double-ball Game was known upon this continent in the remote past.

The peculiar ball employed for this game is composed of two small stuffed pouches connected by a band, or two billets of wood about five inches long, made like thick pegs with heads and ornamented on all sides with carvings; a leather thong five to eight inches long is attached at each end to the neck of each of the two billets. Dr. Culin reports an ingenious specimen made by the Maricopa Indians of Arizona; that double-ball is made from narrow strips of leather braided to form a band, each end of which is enlarged by braiding so as to make a ball, the finished article being about eight inches in length. (*Ibid.*, p. 665, Fig. 882.)

*Properties.* — One double-ball; as many sticks as players; red and yellow head-bands, equal in number, for the two sides of players.

*Directions.* — The double-ball should be made in camp in the following manner: A strip of leather or of strong, closely woven brown cloth from fifteen to twenty inches long. For six inches from both ends the strip should be about seven inches wide; the portion of the strip between these wide ends should be about three inches wide. The wide ends are to form the pouches, and the narrower middle section the band to connect the two pouches. The two edges of the strip should be lapped and strongly sewed the entire length of the strip, except a small opening about an inch long left on the side of each of the pouches. Through this opening the pouches are filled with dry sand, then the edges are securely sewed together so that no sand can escape. These pouches are the "balls." The sides of the pouches should be decorated with designs painted in bright colors and a little tuft or tassel of red yarn fastened at the middle of the bottom of the pouch. The sticks should be about thirty-two inches long, not too heavy and somewhat pointed at one end that is slightly curved. Each stick should be marked by an individual device so that it can be claimed by its owner.

Two wickets, made by crotched poles about five and a half to six feet high, having a bar fastened across the top, are placed in line with each other, one at the East, the other at the West, and as far apart as the limits of the camp grounds will permit. A red streamer to be tied to the eastern wicket and a yellow streamer to the western wicket.

The players are divided into two parties of equal numbers and lots should be drawn to decide which side shall have the eastern goal, and all of that side must wear red head-bands; the other side must wear yellow head-bands to show that theirs is the western goal.

An Umpire must be chosen, to whom belongs the duty of tossing the ball when necessary; to keep the score, and to settle any disputes.

To make a point the ball must be tossed so as to hang on the crossbar of the wicket. An agreement must be made as to how many points shall constitute the game.

## THE GAME

The players stand in two rows about fifteen to twenty feet apart, one color on one side, the other color opposite. The Umpire takes a place between the two lines and as near as possible to the middle of the rows. When all are in readiness the double-ball is tossed by the Umpire straight up into the air, and all those whose places are near the middle of the rows watch the descent of the "ball" and try to catch on their sticks the connecting cord of the double-ball. If one succeeds, she tries to send it down the line toward the goal of her side; those of the opposite side try to prevent success to this movement and to send the "ball" in the other direction. The "ball" should not be allowed to touch the ground from the time it is tossed until it is lodged on the wicket. The side that lets the "ball" fall to the ground loses a count, and the side that keeps the "ball" up until it reaches the goal scores two points, equal to four counts.

## HOOP AND JAVELIN

INTRODUCTORY NOTE. — This game was widely known and played among the various tribes dwelling within the territory now occupied by the United States. In its passage from one tribe to another the game became modified into several types, but the fundamental character was not changed, so that all these types are, in a sense, a unit. The game is very old upon this land; the articles used in playing it have been found in ancient graves, in the cliff dwellings of the Southwest and in various ruins scattered over the country.

Among the Pueblo tribes the articles used in types of this game appear among the paraphernalia on altars prepared for certain ceremonies. From a study of these ceremonies in connection with the myths of the people it seems probable that the hoop used in this game represents the shield of the War God. When the hoop has a netting that fills the center and covers the edges, the netting simulates the magic web of the Spider Woman, a person that frequently figures in the myths and stories of different tribes. Her web generally serves as a protection furnished by her in a conflict.

The netted hoop appears as a decoration upon the interior of pottery bowls formerly made by the Indians of the Southwest. In some of these bowls the netting is dotted with spots. Dr. Culin regards this particular design "as representing the spider web with the dew upon it," and adds: "The 'water shield' [of one of the Zuñi War Gods], from which he shook the torrents, was suggested, no doubt, by dew on the web." (*Ibid.*, p. 425.) To one unfamiliar with the Indian's habit of mind it may seem strained to connect the beads of dew on a spider's web with the torrential rain, but to one familiar with native thought as expressed in myths where the Indian has dramatized his conceptions of nature and of natural forces and phenomena, the connection ceases to be strange.

On the Pueblo altars the netted shield is always associated with arrows, bows or darts. In the various types of this game the arrows, darts, bows, javelins and lances that are associated with the hoop are interchangeable, some tribes using one and other tribes another. Under all the varied types with their different forms as found among scattered and unrelated tribes the game holds to its original significance, primarily religious in character, being an appeal for the protection and the perpetuity of life.

Only two articles are required for this game, the hoop and the javelin.    In one type the hoop is covered with a netting more or less closely and elaborately woven.    In all the netted designs it is usually possible to trace a figure as of a path crossing at right angles in the center of the space within the hoop and ending at four equidistant points on the edge of the hoop.    This path indicates the path of the Four Winds, which stand with their life-giving power at the four directions, the North, East, South and West.    In some localities the netting of the hoop is made from the yucca, in other places corn husks are used.    With the closely netted hoop arrows are apt to be found.    Some of these have as the shaft a corn cob with a stick about eighteen inches long thrust through the cob, sharpened at the lower end and a tuft of feathers tied to the upper end; this feathered stick is a prayer-stick such as is offered at a shrine.

In another type of the game the hoop is of stone; the lance is associated with this kind of hoop.

There are a variety of nettings for the hoop and much diversity in the style of arrows, darts and javelins used in the game.

The simplest is chosen to be here presented, for the reason that both the articles used in the game should be made in the camp where it is to be played.    The hoop and javelins were always made by the youths who joined

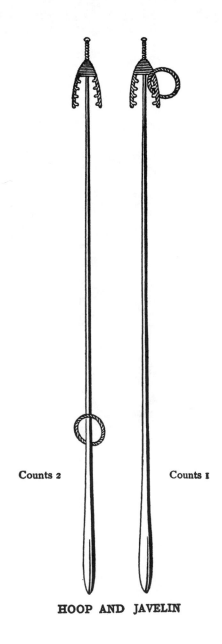

Counts 2                    Counts 1

HOOP AND JAVELIN

in the sport, and the making of hoop and javelin was part of the fun.

*Properties.* — A hoop and two javelins.

The hoop is made in the following manner: A piece of rope, not of a heavy kind, about sixteen inches long will give the foundation for a hoop about four inches in diameter. The two ends should be spliced together so as to leave the edge of the hoop even. The ring of rope is wound with a strip of leather or cloth in order to give the hoop such a surface that it can roll and yet be flexible and light.

The javelin is made of three parts, the shaft and the two barbs. The shaft is of wood, four feet long, round and smooth. An inch from one end a section three inches long is cut into both sides of the shaft a quarter of an inch deep, and the bottom and sides made smooth. The barbs are formed from two small branches cut from a tree or shrub so as to preserve three inches of the stem from which the branch forks; the branch is cut so as to be five inches long and is made flat on the inner side. The stem is made flat on both sides; a flange is made on the outer side. Several pieces of leather are cut, a quarter of an inch wide and an inch long; these are bound for half their length to the inner and flat side of the branch so as to leave the ends free, which are bent up and stand like teeth along the barb. The stems of the barbs are now fitted into the sections cut on both sides of the shaft so that the barbs point backward on each side of the shaft, and are firmly bound in place on the shaft. About three inches from the other end of the shaft a band is cut around the shaft but not very deeply. The two javelins are made as nearly alike as possible in justice to the players.

*Directions.* — A level course from North to South and from fifty to one hundred feet long. Four players; two stand at the north end of the course and two at the south end. The one whose place is toward the East on the north and the one who stands toward the East on the south end are partners. Both of these players should wear a red band about the head, as red is the color of the East. The two players who stand toward the West at the two ends are partners, and these should wear yellow bands about their heads, yellow being the color of the West. The opponents in the game, therefore, stand side by side. Partners cannot help each other in the playing, but both players count for their side all the points they make.

The javelin is grasped by the middle, the barbed end toward the back, and the plain rounded end is shot toward the hoop.

The number of points that will constitute the game should be decided upon before beginning the game. Ten is the usual number among the Indians. Lots should be drawn as to which of the four players should be the first to throw the hoop. The one who draws the hoop then takes one of the javelins, and the player whose place is beside him takes the other javelin.

## THE GAME

At a signal, the players with the javelins and the hoop start on a run along the course; the one with the hoop throws it a little upward with all his force and both players watch the course of the hoop, having their javelins ready to hurl at the hoop the instant they think they can reach it.   If the javelin passes through the hoop and stops it so that it falls on the shaft below the band that was cut thereon, that throw counts two.   If the hoop is caught on one of the barbs, that counts one. If the shaft goes entirely through the hoop so that it does not fall on the javelin, that counts nothing.   If both javelins catch on the hoop, that is a draw and neither player can count the point made.   If on this run and throwing of the hoop and javelins neither of the players scores a count, the player at the other end who is the partner of the one who threw the hoop now takes the hoop to throw it.   He and his opponent who stands beside him now start on a run; the hoop is thrown and the javelins hurled as before.   In this way the players at the ends of the course alternate in throwing the hoop North or South, but the right to throw the hoop belongs to the player who makes the best point.   The hoop thus passes from the east or west players according to the points made.

The game is an athletic sport, and much skill can be developed in the throwing of the javelins and also in the tossing of the hoop so as to prevent scoring by the opponent.

If the grounds are large enough, there is nothing to prevent having two courses and two games going on at the same time.

## Follow My Leader

This game is widely played among the Indian tribes, particularly by the boys, and also by the girls. The Leader improvises the steps and the movements, which all who follow must repeat and keep time to the song. The song here given is traditional in the Omaha tribe. It has been handed down from one generation of young folk to another — for how many, "nobody knows."

## The Game

A Leader is chosen, and all who join in the game must go where he goes, dance as he dances, move the arms, hands and feet as he does. The skipping and dancing must be in exact time with the song that all must sing. The game gives opportunity for fancy steps, winding, intricate figures, "cutting capers" and merry pranks.

### Song

Follow my Leader where'er he goes;
What he'll do next, nobody knows.

Fol - low my Lead -er    wher - e'er he   goes;

What   he'll   do next,    no - bod - y   knows.

# PART III

## INDIAN NAMES

## INDIAN NAMES

INTRODUCTION. — Among the Indian tribes of the United States all personal names have a definite significance. Although there are diversities in the customs relating to names among the various tribes, yet, looking at these as a whole, personal names are observed to fall generally into two classes: First, those which refer to sacred rites; second, those which commemorate a personal achievement.

An Indian tribe is composed of a number of kinship groups or clans. To each one of these, speaking generally, belongs the hereditary duty of performing a certain rite and also the care of the sacred objects connected with that rite. Each kinship group or clan has a set of personal names, all of which refer to the rite peculiar to the clan, or to the sacred objects or to the symbols connected with the rite, and one of these names is given to each person born within the clan. Names of this class are generally retained by men and women throughout life and, to a degree, are regarded as sacred in character. These names have also a social significance, as they always indicate the birth status of the person, for the name at once shows to which clan or kinship group the bearer belongs. No one can exchange his clan or birth name, any more than he can change his sex.

The names that belong to the second class are those which are taken by an adult to mark an achievement. This must be an act in which he has shown special ability or courage in successfully defending his people

from danger.  Such a name, therefore, marks an epoch
in a man's life and is strictly personal to the man, and,
to a degree, indicative of his character or attainments.
It sometimes happens, although but rarely, that a man
on such an occasion may decide to take the name of a
noted ancestor rather than acquire an entirely new
name, but the character of the act of taking a new name
is not thereby changed.

These facts concerning the significance of Indian
personal names throw light on the widespread custom
observed among Indians of never addressing men or
women by their personal names or of using those
names in their presence.  To do so is a breach of good
manners.  The personal name, as has been shown,
refers either to the religious rites sacred to the bearer's
clan or else to a notable act performed by the man; in
both cases the name stands for something that is too
closely connected with the life of the individual to
make it fit for common use.  The difficulty of designat-
ing a person one wishes to address is met by the use of
terms of relationship.  Of course, in some companies
these terms would be literally true and proper, but there
are terms which are used in a wider sense and which
do not imply actual kinship.  (The subject of Indian
relationships and their terms is too complex to be entered upon here.)  There are terms which are employed
merely to indicate respect.  For instance, "Grand-
father" is used when addressing or speaking of the
President of the United States; "Little Father" and
"Father" when addressing or speaking of the Secretary
of the Interior and the Commissioner of Indian Affairs,

both of whom rank below the President, as is well known to the Indian.    The use of terms of relationship may appear strange to us, but there is, as we have seen, a reason for it.    This reason also explains why a child or an adult generally stands mute when we address him by his personal name or ask him what his name is; his silence is not to be attributed to "Indian stolidity," which we ignorantly regard as a marked characteristic of the race.

The bestowal of a name, whether the name is of the first or of the second class already described, was always attended with ceremonies.    These differed among the many tribes of the United States, particularly in their details, but fundamentally they had much in common.

### Presenting the Child to the Cosmos

Among the Omaha a ceremony was observed shortly after the birth of a child that on broad lines reflects a general belief among the Indians.

In the introductory chapter of this book the Indian's feeling of unquestioning unity with nature is mentioned. The following Omaha ceremony and ritual furnish direct testimony to the profundity of this feeling. Its expression greets him at his birth and is iterated at every important experience throughout his life.

When an Omaha child is born the parents send to the clan that has charge of the rite of introducing the child to the Cosmos. The priest thus summoned comes to the tent wherein the infant lies and takes his stand just outside the door, facing the East. He raises his right hand, palm outward, to the sky, and in a clear ringing voice intones the following ritual:

Ho! Ye Sun, Moon, Stars, all ye that move in the heavens,
I bid you hear me!
Into your midst has come a new life;
Consent ye, I implore!
Make its path smooth, that it may reach the brow of the first hill!

Ho! Ye Winds, Clouds, Rain, Mist, all ye that move in the air,
I bid you hear me!
Into your midst has come a new life;
Consent ye, I implore!
Make its path smooth, that it may reach the brow of the second hill!

Ho! Ye Hills, Valleys, Rivers, Lakes, Trees, Grasses, all ye of
the earth,
I bid you hear me!
Into your midst has come a new life;
Consent ye, I implore!
Make its path smooth, that it may reach the brow of the third
hill!

Ho! Ye Birds, great and small, that fly in the air;
Ho! Ye Animals, great and small, that dwell in the forests;
Ho! Ye Insects that creep among the grasses and burrow in the
ground,
I bid you hear me!
Into your midst has come a new life;
Consent ye, I implore!
Make its path smooth, that it may reach the brow of the
fourth hill!

Ho! All ye of the heavens, all ye of the air, all ye of the earth,
I bid you hear me!
Into your midst has come a new life;
Consent ye, consent ye all, I implore!
Make its path smooth — then shall it travel beyond the four
hills!

In this manner the child, the "new life," was introduced to the Cosmos of which it was now a part. All
the powers of the heavens and of the earth were invoked to render aid to the "new life" in its onward
struggle over the rugged path that traverses the four
hills of life, typifying Infancy, Youth, Maturity and
Old Age.

An infant was merely a "new life," it was wholly dependent upon others; no name was given it (only endearing terms were used), for the reason that a name implies either a sacred responsibility or a personal achievement, neither of which was possible to an infant.  When, however, the child could go about alone, generally at three or four years of age, the time had arrived when it must be given a tribal name, one belonging to the rites in charge of its birth group.  By means of this ceremonial act the child was inducted by sacred rites into the tribe and became a recognized member.

### GIVING THE CHILD A NAME

This ceremony, formerly practiced among the Omaha and cognate tribes, took place in the spring, "when the grass was up and the birds were singing." A tent was set apart and made sacred by the priest who had the hereditary right to perform the ceremony. As the occasion was one of tribal interest, many people flocked to the scene of the rite.

A large stone was brought and placed on the east side of the fire that was burning in the center of the space inside the tent. When everything was ready the old priest stood at the door awaiting the arrival of the child. Then all the mothers who had children of the proper age wended their way to this tent, each one leading her little child, who carried in its hands a new pair of moccasins. As the two reached the tent the mother addressed the priest, saying: "Venerable man, I desire my child to wear moccasins." (This was a symbolic form of expression.) "I desire my child to walk long upon the earth, to be content with the light of many days. We seek your protection!" The priest made a formal reply and the little one, carrying its moccasins, entered the tent alone. After a few ritualistic phrases the priest accompanied the child to the fire place, where he and the child stood facing the East while the priest sang an invocation to the Four Winds. He bade them to come hither and stand in this place in four groups.

At the close of this Ritual Song the priest lifted the child by the arms so that its little bare feet rested upon the stone, as it faced the South; then he lifted the

child again by the arms and its feet rested on the stone,
as it faced the West; again the child was lifted and its
feet were upon the stone, as it faced the North; once
more the priest lifted the child and its feet touched the
stone, as it faced the East.  Then the priest sang the
following Ritual Song:

> Turned by the Winds goes the one I send yonder,
> Yonder he goes who is whirled by the Winds,
> Goes where the four hills of life and the Four Winds
>     are standing,
> There into the midst of the Winds do I send him,
> Into the midst of the Winds standing there!

This song and the entire ceremony, which is spoken of
as "Turning the child," are highly symbolic and cannot
be fully explained at this time.  The Winds are the
messengers of the great invisible Wakon'da and bring
the breath of life and strength to man.  At the close
of this song the priest put the new moccasins on the feet
of the child and sang another Ritual Song which says:

> Here unto you has been spoken the truth;
> Because of this truth you shall stand.
> Here declared is the truth;
> Here in this place has been shown you the truth.
> Therefore, arise!  Go forth in its strength!

As the priest sang the last line he set the child on
its feet and made it take four steps toward the East;
these steps are typical of its now entering into life.
Then the priest led the child to the entrance of the

tent, where he called aloud the tribal name of the child, then for the first time proclaimed, adding:

"Ho! Ye Hills, ye Grass, ye Trees, ye creeping things, both great and small, I bid you hear! This child has thrown away its baby name!  Ho!"

All the children of the tribe passed through this ceremony and in this way received their sacred personal names, which were never dropped throughout their after-life, not even when a man took a new name.

### Bestowing a New Name

The bestowal of a new name upon an adult generally took place at some tribal ceremony when all the people were gathered together. In this way as much publicity as possible was given to the act. Among the Pawnee tribe there were three requirements that had to be met in order to take a new name:

First, a man could only take a new name after the performance of an act indicative of ability or strength of character;

Second, the name had to be assumed openly in the presence of the people to whom the act it commemorated was known;

Third, it was necessary that it should be announced in connection with such a ritual as that here given.

These three requirements indicate (1) that a man's name stood for what he had shown himself to be by the light of his actions; (2) that this was recognized by his tribesmen, and (3) that it was proclaimed by one having charge of mediatory rites through which man can be approached by the supernatural.

The old priest who gave the following ritual and explained it said: "A man's life is an onward movement. If one has within him a determined purpose and seeks the help of the powers, his life will climb up." Here he made a gesture indicating a line slanting upward; then he arrested the movement and, still holding his hand where he had stopped, went on to say: "As a man is climbing up, he does something that marks a place in his life where the powers have given him an opportunity to express in acts his peculiar endowments; so this place, this act, forms a stage in his career and he takes a new name to indicate that he is on a level different from that he occupied previously." He added: "Some men can rise only a little way, others live on a dead level." He illustrated his words by moving his hands horizontally. "Men having power to advance climb step by step." Again he made his meaning clear by outlining a flight of steps.

The following ritual is recited on the occasion of taking a new name and is a dramatic poem in three parts. The first gives briefly the institution of the rite of changing one's name in consequence of a new achievement; the second shows how the man was enabled to accomplish this act. It begins with his lonely vigil and fast when he cried to the powers for help; the scene then shifts to the circle of the lesser powers, who, in council, deliberate on his petition which makes its way to them and finally wins their consent; then the winds summon the messengers and these, gathering at the command of the lesser powers, are sent to earth to the man crying in lonely places, to grant him his desire. This part closes with a few vivid words which set forth that only by the favor of the powers had the man been able to do the deed. The third part deals with the man's names — the one to be discarded and the one now to be assumed. The ritual is in rhythmic form, impossible to reproduce in English. The following rendition contains nothing which is not in the original text as explained and amplified by the priest.

The ritual was intoned in a loud voice; the man who

was to receive a new name stood before the priest where he could be seen by the entire assembly.

Harken!  'Twas thus it came to pass:
    In ancient days, a Leader and his men
    Walked this wide earth, man's vast abode
    Roofed by the heavens, where dwell the gods.
    They reached a place the spot no man can tell,
    Faced dangers dread and vanquished them;
    Then, standing as if born anew to life,
    Each warrior threw away the name
    That had been his ere yet these deeds were done.

Harken!  The Leader and his men
    Made there the Vict'ry song, and set the mark
    Ye must o'ertake, if ye would be like them!

Harken!  The Leader and his men
    Turned then toward home.  Their Vict'ry song
    Proclaimed them near;  the village rose,
    Looked toward the hill, where on the top
    Stood the brave men, singing their song,
    Heralding thus the favor of the gods
    By which they had surpassed all former deeds —
    Made new their claim to be accounted men.

Harken!  And whence, think ye, was borne
    Unto these men courage to dare,
    Strength to endure hardship and war?
    Mark well my words, as I reveal
    How the gods help man's feebleness.
    The Leader of these warriors was a man
    Given to prayer.  Oft he went forth

Seeking a place no one could find.
There would he stand and lift his voice,
Fraught with desire that he might be
Invincible, a bulwark 'gainst all foes
Threat'ning his tribe, causing them fear.
Night-time and day this cry sped on,
Traveling far, seeking to reach —
Harken! Those places far above,
Harken! Within the circle vast
Where sit the gods watching o'er men.

Harken! This poor man's prayer went on,
Speeding afar into the blue
Heavens above, reached there the place —
Harken! Where dwell the lesser gods,
Harken! And great Ti-ra'-wa, mightier than all!

Harken! It was because a god
Received this prayer, considered it,
Favored its plea, and passed it on
To him whose place was next, in that grand ring,
Who in his turn received the prayer, .
Considered it, and sent it on —
Harken! Around that circle vast,
Harken! Where sit the gods above.

Harken! And thus it was the prayer
Sent by this man won the consent
Of all the gods. For each god in his place
Speaks out his thought, grants or rejects
Man's suppliant cry, asking for help;
But none can act until the Council grand
Comes to accord, thinks as one mind,
Has but one will all must obey.

Harken!   The Council gave consent;
Harken!   And great Ti-ra'-wa, mightier than all!

Harken!   To make their purpose known,
    Succor and aid freely to give,
    Heralds were called, called by the Winds.
    Then in the West uprose the Clouds
    Heavy and black, ladened with storm.
    Slowly they climbed, dark'ning the skies,
    While close on every side the Thunders marched
    On their dread way, till all were come
    To where the gods in stately council sat
    Waiting for them.   Then bade them go
    Back to the earth, carrying aid
    To him whose prayer had reached their circle vast.
    This mandate given, the Thunders turned toward earth,
    Taking their course slantwise the sky.

Harken!   Another followed hard —
    Lightning broke forth out of the cloud,
    Zigzag and dart, cleaving their way
    Slantwise to earth, their goal to reach.

Harken!   For these two were not all
    That hastened to proclaim the god's behest —
    Swift on their wings Swallows in flocks
    Swept in advance, ranging the path,
    Black breasts and Red, Yellow and White,
    Flying about, clearing the way
    For those who bore the message of the gods
    Granting the man courage to dare,
    Strength to endure, power to stand
    Invincible, a bulwark 'gainst all foes.

Harken! 'Twas thus it came to pass:
    The Leader grasped the help sent by the gods;
    Henceforth he walked steadfast and strong,
    Leading his men through dangers drear,
    Knowing that naught could strike at him
    To whom the gods had promised victory.

Attend! Once more I change his name.

Harken! *Ri-ruts'-ka-tit* it was
    We used to call him by, a name he won
    Long days ago, marking an act
    Well done by him, but now passed by.

Harken! To-day all men shall say —

Harken! His act has lifted him
    Where all his tribe behold a man
    Clothed with new fame, strong in new strength
    Gained by his deeds, blessed of the gods.
Harken! *Sha-ku'-ru Wa'-ruk-ste* shall he be called.

### Taking an Indian Name in Camp

In view of the significance of Indian personal names, and the dignity and reverence which in every instance surrounded the giving or the taking of a name, it hardly seems appropriate that Indian names should be assumed even for a short period without some regard being shown to the customs and thought of the people from whom the names are borrowed. While there should be no travesty of rites such as those that have been here described, rites that have been held sacred upon this continent for untold generations, still it would not be unseemly to hold to the spirit of those rites when we borrow these names during the camp days in which we seek to live close to the nature that the Indian loved so reverently and well.

When it is decided among the members of the camp to take an Indian name, on the day of the ceremony all the camp should assemble early in the morning. When all have gathered, they should move toward a place where the sun can be seen when it rises over the lake, the hilltops or the woods.   There all should pause.

The candidate for the name should not wear any head-band.  The boy or girl should stand well to the front of the group, all of whom should face the East. The entire company should then join in the following song:

## Song No. 1

Skies proclaim a new day!  We joyfully meet,
We thankfully greet,
His* new name this day shall repeat.

The Leader of the camp must then intone the following:

Hear! O Trees that gird our camp!
Listen, ye Birds that fly through the branches!
Harken, ye rippling waves on Stream and Lake!
Hear me!
Into your midst has come a friend,
He* bears a new Name!
Ye shall know him as ————— (name)

The announcement of the name should be distinctly made so as to be clearly heard by the entire company. The head-band or other camp insignia should now be officially put on the candidate.

All present should then join in singing the following song, clapping their hands as beats to the music as they skip back to breakfast and to the pleasures of the day:

---

*The pronoun should be changed according to the sex of the candidate.

## Song No. 2

Homeward we go, calling his* name;
New is the name now we proclaim;
No other change in our friend, he* is the same!

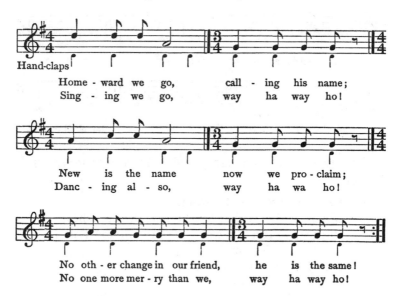

Hand-claps

Home - ward we    go,        call - ing    his    name;
Sing - ing  we    go,        way    ha    way    ho!

New      is   the   name         now    we  pro - claim;
Danc - ing  al - so,            way    ha    wa    ho!

No  oth - er change in  our friend,      he      is   the same!
No  one more mer - ry than  we,          way    ha  way ho!

**2**

Singing we go, way ha way ho!
Dancing also, way ha way ho!
No one more merry than we, way ha way ho!

The second stanza should be repeated and the steps
kept in rhythm until the dancers finally disperse.

---

* Change the pronoun to the proper sex.

## INDIAN NAMES FOR BOYS

All vowels have the Continental sound

The names here presented, for Boys, for Girls and for Camps, have been chosen out of many because the words are easily pronounced; none of them have any of the peculiar labial, nasal or guttural sounds common in the various Indian languages, which are difficult to represent by the letters of our alphabet and equally difficult for most Americans to pronounce.

| | | | |
|---|---|---|---|
| 1. | A-di'-ta | Priest | Omaha. |
| 2. | An'-ge-da | From every direction | Omaha. |
| 3. | De'-mon-thin | Talks as he walks | Ponca. |
| 4. | E-di'-ton | Standing as a sacred object | Omaha. |
| 5. | Ga-he'-ge | Chief | Omaha. |
| 6. | Gu'-da-hi | "There he goes!" A coyote | Omaha. |
| 7. | Ha'-nu-ga-hi | Nettle weed | Ponca. |
| 8. | He'-ba-zhu | Little horns | Ponca. |
| 9. | He'-ga | Buzzard | Omaha. |
| 10. | He'-sha-be | Dark antlers | Omaha. |
| 11. | He'-thon-ton | Towering antlers (elk) | Omaha. |
| 12. | Ho-ho' | Fish | Omaha. |
| 13. | Hon'-ga | Imperial eagle | Osage. |
| 14. | Hu'-ton-ton | Roar of thunder | Omaha. |
| 15. | I'-ku-ha-be | He who causes fear | Ponca. |
| 16. | I-shta'-pe-de | Fire eyes (lightning) | Ponca. |
| 17. | Ka-ge'-zhin-ga | Little brother | Omaha. |
| 18. | Ka-wa'-ha | Very old name, meaning lost | Omaha. |
| 19. | Ka'-wa-sab-be | Black horse | Osage. |
| 20. | Ka'-wa-ska | White horse | Osage. |
| 21. | Ka'-wa-zi | Yellow horse | Osage. |
| 22. | Ke'-ton-ga | Great turtle | Ponca. |
| 23. | Ke'-zhin-ga | Little turtle | Ponca. |
| 24. | Ki'-ko-ton-ga | Curlew | Omaha. |
| 25. | Ki'-mon-hon | Facing the wind | Omaha. |

| 26. | Ki'-wa-go | Male buffalo | Pawnee. |
|---|---|---|---|
| 27. | Ku'-ge | Sound of the drum | Omaha. |
| 28. | Ku'-rux | Bear | Pawnee. |
| 29. | Ku'-sox | Left hand | Pawnee. |
| 30. | Le-sha'-ro | Chief | Pawnee. |
| 31. | Mi'-da-in-ga | Playful sun | Osage. |
| 32. | Mi'-ka | Raccoon | Ponca. |
| 33. | Mi'-ka-si | Coyote | Omaha. |
| 34. | Min'-dse | Bow | Osage. |
| 35. | Mon-chu' | Bear | Omaha. |
| 36. | Mon-chu'-pa | Bear's head | Omaha. |
| 37. | Mon-e'-ga-he | Arrow chief | Ponca. |
| 38. | Mon-ge'-zi | Yellow breast | Omaha. |
| 39. | Mon-ka'-ta | He of the earth | Ponca. |
| 40. | Mon'-sa | Arrow shaft | Osage. |
| 41. | Mon'-te-ga | New arrows | Osage. |
| 42. | Ni-ni'-ba | Pipe | Omaha. |
| 43. | Ni'-sho-sho | Swallow | Omaha. |
| 44. | Non-ke'-ne | Graceful walker (deer) | Omaha. |
| 45. | Non'-nun-ge | Runner | Osage. |
| 46. | Non'-pe-wa-the | He who is feared | Omaha. |
| 47. | Nu'-da-hun-ga | Captain | Omaha. |
| 48. | O'-pa | Elk | Omaha. |
| 49. | Pa-he'-ta-pe | Seeking the hills | Omaha. |
| 50. | Pa'-na-hoo | Owl | Omaha. |
| 51. | Pa'-sun | American eagle | Omaha. |
| 52. | Pa-thon' | White-headed eagle | Omaha. |
| 53. | Pe'-de-ga-he | Fire chief | Omaha. |
| 54. | Pe'-num-ba | Seven | Ponca. |
| 55. | Sha-ku'-ru | Sun | Pawnee. |
| 56. | Sha-thu' | Sound of the water | Ponca. |
| 57. | Shon'-ge | Wolf | Omaha. |
| 58. | Shon'-ge-sab-be | Black wolf | Omaha. |
| 59. | Shon'-ge-ska | White wolf | Ponca. |

| | | |
|---|---|---|
| 60. Shon'-ge-zi | Yellow wolf | Ponca. |
| 61. Shon'-ton-ga | Grey wolf | Ponca. |
| 62. Sho-sho'-ka | Osprey | Omaha. |
| 63. Shu'-ka-bi | Bunch of clouds | Ponca. |
| 64. Ski'-rik | Grey wolf | Pawnee. |
| 65. Ta-de'-ta | To the wind | Omaha. |
| 66. Ta-de'-u-mon-thin | Walking in the wind | Omaha. |
| 67. Te-thon' | White buffalo | Omaha. |
| 68. The'-ha | Soles | Omaha. |
| 69. U'-ba-ni | Digging in the earth (little creatures) | Omaha. |
| 70. U-ga'-e | Spread out (herd of buffalo) | Omaha. |
| 71. Wa-he'-he | Easy to break, fragile | Omaha. |
| 72. Wa-ke'-de | One who shoots | Omaha. |
| 73. Wa-po'-ga | Grey owl | Omaha. |
| 74. Wa-shis'-ka | Shell | Omaha. |
| 75. Wash-kon'-hi | Power of the thunder | Omaha. |
| 76. Wa-sho'-she | Brave | Omaha. |
| 77. Wa-thu'-he | Startles the game | Omaha. |
| 78. Wa-zhin'-ska | Wisdom | Omaha. |
| 79. We'-kush-ton | One who gives feast frequently | Omaha. |
| 80. Wi'-a-go | Feather | Dakota. |
| 81. Zha'-be | Beaver | Omaha. |

## INDIAN NAMES FOR GIRLS

| | | |
|---|---|---|
| 1. A'-bey | Leaf | Omaha. |
| 2. A'-bey-tu | Green leaf | Omaha. |
| 3. A'-bet-zi | Yellow leaf | Omaha. |
| 4. A'-ka-wi | South wind | Omaha. |
| 5. A-sin'-ka | Youngest daughter | Osage. |
| 6. Chon'-ku-sha | Robin | Dakota. |
| 7. Chon'-wa-pe | Leaf | Dakota. |

| | | | |
|---|---|---|---|
| 8. | Chon'-wa-pe-ska | Red leaf | Dakota. |
| 9. | Chon'-wa-pe-tu | Green leaf | Dakota. |
| 10. | Cho-xon'-zhe-da | Willow | Dakota. |
| 11. | Da'-a-bi | The visible sun | Omaha. |
| 12. | Don'-a-ma | The sun visible to all | Omaha. |
| 13. | Ha'-ba-zhu-dse | Red corn | Osage. |
| 14. | Ha'-ba-zi | Yellow corn | Osage. |
| 15. | Ha'-ba-tu | Blue corn | Osage. |
| 16. | Ha'-ba-ska | White corn | Osage. |
| 17. | Hon'-ba-he | Dawn | Dakota. |
| 18. | I-shta'-sa-pa | Dark eyes | Dakota. |
| 19. | I'-ni-a-bi | Home builder | Omaha. |
| 20. | Ka-shi'-a-ka | Meadow lark | Omaha. |
| 21. | Mi'-a-kon-da | Sacred moon | Omaha. |
| 22. | Mi'-gi-na | Returning moon | Omaha. |
| 23. | Mi'-mi-te | Standing new moon | Omaha. |
| 24. | Mi'-na | Oldest daughter | Osage. |
| 25. | Mi'-pe | Good moon | Omaha. |
| 26. | Mi'-ta-in | Crescent moon | Ponca. |
| 27. | Mi'-the-be | Shadowy moon | Ponca. |
| 28. | Mi'-ton-e | New moon | Omaha. |
| 29. | Mi'-wa-thon | White moon | Omaha. |
| 30. | Ni'-da-wi | Fairy girl | Omaha. |
| 31. | Pa'-zi | Yellow head (bird) | Ponca. |
| 32. | Pa'-ha-zi | Yellow hair (young animal) | Ponca. |
| 33. | Raw-ska' | Anemone | Omaha. |
| 34. | Raw-tu' | Violet | Omaha. |
| 35. | Raw-zi' | Sunflower | Omaha. |
| 36. | Ta'-de-win | Wind maiden | Omaha. |
| 37. | Ta'-in | New moon | Ponca. |
| 38. | Ta'-in-ge | Coming moon | Ponca. |
| 39. | Wa-ha'-ba | Corn | Omaha. |
| 40. | Wa-ha'-ba-ska | White corn | Omaha. |
| 41. | Wa-ha'-ba-tu | Blue corn | Omaha. |

| | | | |
|---|---|---|---|
| 42. | Wa-ha'-ba-zi | Yellow corn | Omaha. |
| 43. | Wak'-cha | Flower | Dakota. |
| 44. | Wak'-cha-zi | Sunflower | Dakota. |
| 45. | Wa-shu'-dse | Wild-rose | Omaha. |
| 46. | Wa-te'-win | Victory woman | Omaha. |
| 47. | Wa-zhin'-ga | Bird | Omaha. |
| 48. | Wa-zhin'-ga-tu | Blue bird | Omaha. |
| 49. | We'-thon-ki-tha | To come together (as in a society) | Omaha. |
| 50. | We'-ton-a | Old name, meaning lost | Omaha. |
| 51. | We'-ton-be-the | One who gives hope | Omaha. |
| 52. | Wi'-he | Younger sister | Omaha. |
| 53. | Wi'-te-ga | New moon | Dakota. |
| 54. | Zit-ka'-la | Bird | Dakota. |
| 55. | Zit-ka'-la-sha | Red bird | Dakota. |
| 56. | Zit-ka'-la-tu | Blue bird | Dakota. |
| 57. | Zit-ka'-la-zi | Yellow bird | Dakota. |

## INDIAN NAMES FOR CAMPS

| | |
|---|---|
| E'-zhon U-ti | A Camp among the Elms. |
| Hin'-de-hi U-ti | A Camp among the Lindens. |
| Ney'-a-ti | A Camp by the Lake. |
| Tosh'-ka-hi U-ti | A Camp among the Oaks. |
| Wa-shis'-ka A-ti | A Camp by the Brook. |